MW01687728

COFFEE CRAZY

A Guide to the 100 Best Coffeehouses in America

by Marybeth Bizjak

Aslan Publishing
Santa Rosa, California

Published by
Aslan Publishing
3356 Coffey Lane
Santa Rosa, CA 95403
(707) 542-5400

Library of Congress Cataloging-in-Publication Data:

Bizjak, Marybeth, 1958-
Coffee crazy : a guide to the 100 best coffeehouses in America / Marybeth Bizjak.
p. cm.
Includes index.
ISBN 0-944031-6-1

1. Coffeehouses—United States—Guidebooks. I. Title

TX907.2.B57 1996 647.9573
QBI96-20151

Copyright ©1996 Marybeth Bizjak

All rights reserved. No part of this publication may be reproduced, stored in a retrieval system, or transmitted in any form or by any means, electronic, mechanical, photocopy, recording, or otherwise, without prior written permission from Aslan Publishing, Santa Rosa, California, USA, with the exception of short excerpts used with acknowledgment of publisher and author.

Cover Design by Steve Graydon
Page Design by Marianne Harris
Set in Souvenir and Lithos
Printed in the USA
First Edition

10 9 8 7 6 5 4 3 2 1

To Tony, with love and gratitude

TABLE OF CONTENTS

SCRUMPTIOUS RECIPES

DISCOVERING THE CAFE EXPERIENCE

INTRODUCTION

When I moved to San Francisco from the East Coast years ago, I had no job, little money and few friends in town. Every afternoon, after spending the day phoning potential employers and sending out resumes, I'd head down the street to a coffeehouse named Peet's, where I'd reward myself with a steaming cappuccino and an hour or two of people watching.

Sitting on a stool by a big plate-glass window, I'd flip through a magazine and ponder my uncertain future. Nearby were others like me, writing, working on laptop computers or talking to their friends.

After spending the day alone in an empty apartment, I felt good simply being around others. No one bothered me or pressured me to move on. For the price of a cup of coffee, I was entertained, relaxed, comforted and connected.

Peet's was a sensual place full of wonderful smells, sounds and sights. Not until much later did I learn that this Berkeley-based coffee roasting company is in fact the granddaddy of America's current cafe boom, serving as a model for gourmet coffee businesses from Seattle to the East Coast. But I caught on instinctively to what was good and right about cafes: I adored the informality, the coziness and homeyness that invited me to linger for hours. And the coffee itself was a revelation: rich, complex and delicious.

I became hooked on the coffeehouse experience.

In the years since, I've made literally thousands of visits to coffeehouses and cafes, and sipped hundreds of coffee blends and styles. I've gone to cafes by myself and with others — friends, dates, co-workers, the man who became my husband, and eventually even our two children. The coffeehouse became my home away from home.

Whenever we travel, my husband (also a cafe aficionado) and I look for a coffeehouse like those we left behind in California. In the past our search was often fruitless: The coffee was poor, the atmosphere unremarkable.

But a couple of years ago, that started to change. We found a wonderful bookstore cafe in a small suburb of Dayton, Ohio. We actually got a decent espresso on a visit to the New Jersey seashore. We discovered several wonderful coffeehouses on a trip to see friends in Washington, D.C.

Coffeehouses have ceased to be a West Coast phenomenon. In fact, America has gone coffee crazy.

But you know that. At this moment you may be sitting at a table in your favorite coffeehouse, sipping a cappuccino or a caffe latte. You are part of America's new Cafe Society, a burgeoning group of people who enjoy the sophisticated pleasure of a simple yet historic ritual.

This book will introduce you to what I consider to be the 100 best coffeehouses in America. I've also included coffeehouse recipes, coffee facts, and profiles of people from all over the country who frequent coffeehouses.

Use *Coffee Crazy* as a travel guide or simply let it inspire your daydreams. Relax, have a sip and enjoy.

THE AMERICANIZATION OF CAFES

Leave it to industrious America to tinker with an ancient tradition: We've made cafe society downright utilitarian.

Sure, many Americans treat their coffeehouses much the same way the Italians, the Austrians and the French have for three centuries: as a reprieve from the world, as a nexus of creativity, and as a milieu for conversation on topics both grand and intimate. Like the French, we go to cafes to while away the hours offering solutions to the problems of the world; like the Viennese we go to relax and regroup; like the Italians, we go to gossip with friends. But many of us have added a particularly American spin to cafe life. We go to the cafe to get things done.

I have a friend who balances his checkbook in his neighborhood cafe. Better there than at home with children underfoot. Several local politicians hear out constituents in that same cafe. Some CEOs have been known to steal away from work to do some serious planning on the latest company project. College students push the tiny tables together and amass chairs for more convivial study sessions than in the university library. For some of us, it's a wonder how we got through the week before cafes came along.

There are cafes with washing machines and dryers. There are cafes that double as record stores. There are carwash cafes. A cafe in New York City offers tarot and palm readings for the mystically inclined. For the fast-paced among us, there are drive-through espresso booths (in the Pacific Northwest they're called Motor Mokas)—often old mini photo stores in mall parking lots.

Then there are the bookstore cafes, some of which allow you to take a book or magazine to your table for a once-over, over coffee, before deciding whether you want to buy it. There are even nightclub cafes and art gallery cafes.

Increasingly, computers with links to the Internet or local bulletin boards are showing up on cafe tables. In Harvard Square, Cybersmith offers customers several dozen stations with the latest software and virtual reality games. Yet, in deference to the real conversational tradition of cafes, they link the computers within the cafe so that you can chat up any interesting-looking cyber-sipper in the room.

The Americanization of coffeehouse society does not stop with the cafe itself. In the rich American theory that more is better, the coffee itself is served with more variety and accoutrements here than ever imagined in Europe, or in the even more ancient locales for public coffee drinking, Northern Africa and the Middle East.

Many American cafes put up to twice as much espresso in a single shot as the time-honored one-and-a-half-ounce European tradition. In most American cafes, you can order your coffee with flavored syrups, with skim milk, topped with cinnamon, nutmeg or chocolate, served with a twist of lemon or a dollop of whipped cream. Some coffeehouses even create elaborate designs—a heart, say, or a rosette—in the crema and foam atop their drinks. They call it Latte Art.

And, whereas most French would find it incredibly gauche, the traditional demitasse has been replaced in many an American's hands by a paper cup, the better to sip in the car on the way to the office.

No doubt some of these new permutations of the American coffeehouse and coffee drink will soon enough pass away, as fads do.

But the basics of what you see here today—gourmet coffee and eclectic cafes—are here to stay, just as they once caught on in Venice, Vienna and Paris.

Leave it to America, with its zestful and experimental twists on an old concept, to turn coffeehouse society into a distinctly American tradition.

GUIDE TO SYMBOLS

TIDBITS

Fast facts about caffeine and its consumption.

QUOTES

Notable quotables from the famous and infamous about their addiction to hot stuff.

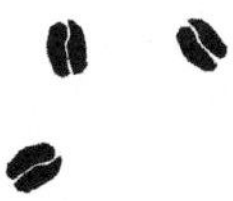

RECIPES

How to recreate cafe comestibles in your own kitchen.

PROFILES

A look at some of the habitues of the nation's coffeehouses.

BEST COFFEEHOUSES ON THE...

EAST COAST

METRO REGIONS

Atlanta
Baltimore
Boston
Charlotte
Miami
New York
Philadelphia
Pittsburgh
Providence
Washington, D.C.

CAFE INTERMEZZO

1845 Peachtree Road
Atlanta, Georgia 30309 • (404) 355-0411
OPEN 10 A.M. TO 3 A.M. SUNDAY TO THURSDAY;
10 A.M. TO 4 A.M. FRIDAY AND SATURDAY.

This cafe in Atlanta's affluent Buckhead neighborhood is open all day, but it's really a late-night hangout. Elegant yet bohemian, Intermezzo has the air of a bustling turn-of-the-century Viennese coffeehouse: classical music and light opera play softly in the background and twinkling lights are reflected in gilded mirrors as aproned waiters take your order at linen-covered tables topped with fresh flowers. The high-ceilinged space is broken up by arches and columns into three rooms: the Bar, the Cafe and the Loggia, with a 10-sided espresso bar that straddles the two front rooms. In front of the bar are dozens of pastries, and a seven-foot-tall brass Gaggia espresso machine, the largest in the world. There's outdoor seating on the sidewalk in front and on the back patio, where a convertible roof, gas heaters and wind curtains enable patrons to sit year round. After 9 p.m. there's usually a waiting list for a table, so come early.

COFFEE: The coffee menu is actually a small book, featuring brewed coffees from local roasters and imported espresso from Lavazza. The brewed coffee is served in an Austrian coffeepot called a Kannschen. They also carry liqueurs, cognacs, single-malt Scotches, ports, wines and imported beers.

FOOD: Intermezzo serves European pastries—croissants, brioche, pithivier—on weekday mornings, as well as brunch (Belgian waffle, eggs Florentine and Benedict, etc.) on weekends. The chef prepares elegant fare for lunch and dinner: grilled asparagus, baked Brie en croute, grilled salmon salad, tuna burger and prosciutto panini are just a few choices. Desserts, which come from local bakers, are European in style: rich Sacher torte, 37 kinds of cheesecake, and Fruitti di Bosco, which teams red and black raspberries and currants with shortbread and vanilla custard.

CLIENTELE: The diverse crowd ranges from professionals to prom goers, with folks dressed in everything from tuxedos to tennis togs. Locals aren't the only ones here; hotel concierges send over a steady stream of travelers.

GALLETTO ESPRESS-OH!

985 Monroe Drive
Atlanta, Georgia 30308 • (404) 724-0204
OPEN 6:30 A.M. TO 11 P.M. MONDAY TO THURSDAY;
6:30 A.M. TO MIDNIGHT FRIDAY;
8 A.M. TO MIDNIGHT SATURDAY;
AND 8 A.M. TO 10 P.M. SUNDAY.

With its soothing color scheme and low-key New Age music playing on the sound system, Galletto is a quiet, comforting place to recharge your batteries. You can sit at the counter and chat with a friendly barista, or find solitude at an old English pub table or on a padded Mission bench against the wall. During the day, the room is flooded with natural light, brightening the tan walls and concrete floor, which has been finished to look like well-worn leather. At night, the lights are dimmed and candles flicker on every table. The cafe, located in a small retail center close to downtown and the central business district, attracts a well-heeled crowd looking for a soothing place to relax. On Sundays, the owners (two women who abandoned corporate careers) change the tempo by playing their favorite music—showtunes by the likes of Judy Garland and Ethel Merman.

COFFEE: An Oregon roaster provides the West Coast blend, which has a smoky French flavor; a local master roaster supplies the rest of the 30 estate varietals sold here. Every day Galletto offers four coffees, which are placed in air pots for customers to serve themselves. The cappuccinos and lattes, made with a smooth espresso, wear showy stiff froths. Galletto also serves Turkish, Cuban and French Quarter coffee.

FOOD: Galletto serves only baked goods, which are supplied by about 20 local bakers. They include bagels, cupcakes, spiced coffee cake, low-fat muffins (peach, apple cinnamon), and regular muffins, including carrot zucchini and sour cream pecan. The luscious desserts include a wonderful triple-layer chocolate walnut banana cake, Southern red velvet cake, lemon cake, triple chocolate overdose cake, apple pie and oversized cookies.

CLIENTELE: Professionals, local residents and students from Georgia Tech and Emory.

JAVA JIVE

790 Ponce de Leon Avenue
Atlanta, Georgia 30306 • (404) 876-6161
CLOSED MONDAY
OPEN 8 A.M. TO 2 P.M. & 6 P.M. TO MIDNIGHT TUESDAY TO FRIDAY;
10 A.M. TO 2:30 P.M. & 6 P.M. TO MIDNIGHT SATURDAY;
10 A.M. TO 2:30 P.M. SUNDAY.

This stylized coffee and dessert cafe in Atlanta's Virginia-Highland neighborhood is a monument to kitchen design of the '30s, '40s and '50s. Furnished authentically with chrome and Formica dinette sets from mid-century, the shop also includes period appliances, utensils, kitchen clocks and advertising signs meticulously collected at flea markets and garage sales. You practically expect to see an aproned Donna Reed wielding the Sunbeam mixer or brewing up a pot of percolator coffee as swing and Big Band music plays in the background. The owners, husband-and-wife team Steven Horwitz and Shira Levetan, created a place that showcases Levetan's dessert-making talents and pays homage to the superior design and craftsmanship of the past: the counter staff whip up creamy milkshakes on a refurbished Hamilton Beach Mix Master from the '30s and grind coffee on an old A&P grinder. On weekends, Java Jive is Atlanta's hot spot for brunch; regulars come for the gingerbread waffle with homemade lemon curd and the superior pancakes.

COFFEE: A Washington state roaster provides the full-bodied, flavorful coffee, which is served in old-fashioned diner china. While espresso drinks are available, the focus here is on traditional brewed coffee. You can also get soda fountain drinks; try the shot and a shake, a cappuccino ice cream milkshake with a shot of espresso.

FOOD: Everything is made on the premises from scratch. In the mornings, there are muffins and croissants, plus waffles, pancakes, omelets, fried matzo, and a double bull's-eye: a fried piece of bread that encircles a fried egg, served with a side of salsa. The lunch and dinner menu includes vegetarian soups, served with a fluffy homemade biscuit, and sandwiches, such as tarragon chicken salad or roasted red pepper with spinach, feta cheese and pesto on a French roll. The sandwiches are served with homemade potato salad or coleslaw. Desserts are luscious: espresso pie, chocolate decadence cake, white chocolate coffee cheesecake, and brownies and ice cream are just a few examples.

CLIENTELE: The crowd here runs the gamut from young to old and includes a heavy sprinkling of students, photographers and artists.

Chocolate Espresso Pie
Java Jive, Atlanta, Georgia

For crust:

1 1/2 cups chocolate cookie crumbs

2 tablespoons sugar

6 tablespoons butter, melted and slightly cooled

For filling:

8 ounces bittersweet chocolate

1 cup heavy cream

1 tablespoon espresso powder dissolved in 1 tablespoon hot water

2 tablespoons coffee liqueur

For topping:

1 cup heavy cream

1/4 cup powdered sugar

1 1/2 teaspoons vanilla extract

grated chocolate for garnish

To make crust:

1. Combine crumbs, sugar and butter in a small bowl and mix well.
2. Press crumb mixture into a 9-inch pie plate and chill for 30 minutes.

To make filling:

1. Melt chocolate and set aside to cool
2. Using an electric mixer, beat the heavy cream until soft peaks form. Add the dissolved espresso powder and liqueur and resume beating until firm but not stiff.
3. Gently fold the chocolate into the cream mixture and spoon filling into the chilled crust. Chill until firm, about 2 hours.

To make topping:

1. Beat cream until soft peaks form.
2. Add sugar and vanilla and beat until firm. Spoon onto chilled pie and sprinkle with grated chocolate.

SAN FRANCISCO COFFEE ROASTING CO.

1192 North Highland Avenue
Atlanta, Georgia 30306 • (404) 876-8816
OPEN 7 A.M. TO 11 P.M. MONDAY TO FRIDAY; 8 A.M. TO MIDNIGHT SATURDAY; 8A.M. TO 11 P.M. SUNDAY.

Co-owner Doug Bond lived and worked as a coffee roaster in California before moving to Atlanta and opening this charming cafe in the trendy Virginia-Highland district. The basement roastery, complete with a cupping room for coffee tastings, fills the neighborhood with the wonderful scent of roasting beans. The ground-floor cafe is located in an old red-brick building with French windows that open up to the sidewalk, where there are benches for customers to sit. Inside, the walls, ceiling and floor are painted in java-related colors: cappuccino for the walls, coffee for the ceiling, and milk foam for the faux-finished concrete floor. There's a semi-circular mahogany bar where brass coffee bins gleam, and a brick wall inset with a stained-glass window.

COFFEE: The coffee is roasted on-site, and each day there are three blends available: a medium, a dark and a decaf. The cappuccinos and lattes are served in lovely mugs and bowls hand-thrown by a local artist.

FOOD: The cafe carries only pastries and desserts supplied by local bakers. You'll find bear claws, filled croissants, scones and low-fat muffins. Cakes include an awesome blueberry torte, carrot cake, German chocolate cake and Bailey's Irish Cream pie.

CLIENTELE: The lively mix includes kids on in-line skates, bike or foot; young couples with kids; yuppies, and gays and lesbians who live in the neighborhood.

THE DAILY GRIND

1726 Thames Street
Baltimore, Maryland 21231 • (410) 558-0399
OPEN 7:30 A.M. TO 12:30 A.M. SUNDAY TO THURSDAY;
7:30 A.M. TO 2:30 A.M. FRIDAY AND SATURDAY.

This cafe in Fell's Point, a grungy, harbor-front neighborhood, was Baltimore's first specialty coffeehouse, opening in 1992. Located in a picturesque 1850s stable that once housed trolley horses, it features exposed joists and whitewashed walls of brick, stone and mortar. Underfoot are cobblestones, and customers must walk over an enormous antique wooden scale set into the floor to get to the counter and seating area. The cafe gets a steady stream of actors, directors and TV technicians from NBC's *Homicide,* which is filmed nearby.

COFFEE: Owner David Key roasts the excellent coffee himself twice a week. He offers four choices per day, including the house blend, a varietal, a flavor of the day (usually hazelnut) and house decaf. There's a special cafe drink (such as a double raspberry cappuccino) that changes weekly.

FOOD: The coffee is the thing here, so food takes a definite back seat. You'll find baked goods, pastries and candies, all from outside sources. At lunch there's a hummus sandwich.

CLIENTELE: This used to be a favorite of the pierced and dyed set, but the cafe now attracts a more mainstream crowd. There are young professionals, tourists, college kids from Johns Hopkins and Towson State Universities, and celebrities, including actress Jody Foster and *Homicide's* director Barry Levinson and star Andre Braugher.

DONNA'S COFFEE BAR

2 West Madison Street
Baltimore, Maryland 21201 • (410) 385-0180
OPEN 8 A.M. TO 11 P.M. MONDAY TO THURSDAY;
8 A.M. TO 1 A.M.FRIDAY; 10 A.M. TO 1 A.M. SATURDAY;
10 A.M. TO 11 P.M. SUNDAY.

Located in a 150-year-old red-brick building in the historic Mount Vernon district, Donna's is known for its fabulous food and European ambiance. The space is great looking: old on the outside, hip urban contemporary on the inside, it's Baltimore's take on a New York Soho cafe. And at night, the view of the lights from nearby Washington Monument is breathtaking. On the room's right is a concrete bar studded with colorful pieces of glass, where customers place their orders before 11 a.m.; after 11, sit at a table and the staff will wait on you. For the last couple of years, *Baltimore* magazine and the alternative *City Paper* have showered Donna's with awards for both its coffee (roasted by secret suppliers in town and on the West Coast) and its food, which is prepared by talented chef/co-owner Donna Crivello.

COFFEE: Four brewed coffees daily from a local roaster, plus wonderful espresso from a supplier in San Francisco.

FOOD: In the morning, there are butter scones, raisin-walnut bread and muffins, all made from scratch on the premises. On weekends, Donna's serves a frittata, sometimes made with roasted red peppers and leeks, other times with blue crab, a Maryland specialty. The cafe also serves soups, salads and sandwiches, including the popular roasted-vegetable sandwich on olive bread. The decadent desserts include bread pudding, tiramisu, and a cream cheese tart with seasonal fruit.

CLIENTELE: Donna's is a gathering point for local business people, residents and local foodies. It also gets a good museum and post-theater crowd from nearby Center Stage, Peabody Conservatory, Walters Art Gallery and the Maryland Institute of Art.

Donna's Tiramisu
Donna's Coffee Bar, Baltimore, Maryland

36 Italian ladyfingers
2 1/2 cups hot espresso
(you may use instant espresso)
1/4 cup sugar
1/4 cup brandy
2 tablespoons vanilla extract
8 ounces mascarpone (Italian cream cheese)
8 ounces heavy whipping cream
2 tablespoons sifted confectioner's sugar
cocoa powder for garnish

1. Line a 9-by-12-inch pan with 2 layers of ladyfingers, alternating the direction of each layer.
2. Dissolve sugar into hot espresso. Add brandy and vanilla.
3. Pour espresso mixture over ladyfingers and let sit until ladyfingers absorb the liquid.
4. Mix heavy cream and mascarpone in a mixing bowl. Add confectioner's sugar and whip until the cream forms soft peaks. Do not overbeat.
5. Spread the cream mixture evenly over the espresso-soaked ladyfingers. Chill at least two hours.
6. To serve, dust the top with cocoa powder and cut into 3-by-4-inch squares.

Boston commuters have taken drive-through coffee a step further. An entrepreneurial guy named Chris Costonis, aka the Coffee Buster, serves "the world's fastest cup of coffee" to commuters passing through the Sumner Tunnel Toll Plaza during rush hour. It takes him five seconds to serve it black, seven seconds with cream. He stores the coffee in an urn strapped to his back.

BEANS

1655 Beacon Street
Brookline, Massachusetts 02146 • (617) 277-5282
OPEN 7 A.M. TO 9 P.M. MONDAY TO THURSDAY; 7 A.M. TO 11 P.M. FRIDAY AND SATURDAY; 8 A.M. TO 7 P.M. SUNDAY.

Beans is a beauty of a coffeehouse that roasts its own coffee and bakes its own wonderful pastries right in the store. Located in Washington Square, a 15-minute trolley ride from downtown Boston, this upscale eatery has a bright, modern feel, from the black metal pastry cases and hanging bread racks made by a local sculptor to the mahogany and metal tables that fill the spacious, light-filled dining area. Above the service counter hang whimsical paper sculptures, like the one of a businessman running and clutching a cup of coffee as his briefcase flies open, spilling its contents. The coffee beans sit in glass fish tanks along the back wall near a gleaming blue Diedrich coffee roaster, and an extensive selection of loose-leaf teas is displayed in beautiful stainless steel canisters along the wall. Everywhere there is an abundance of food: a big bowl of homemade biscotti on the counter, loaves of bread hanging from the ceiling, and display cases crammed with goodies. Beans also carries an excellent selection of pottery for sale—not just the usual mugs and cups, but artful handmade and production pieces from France, Italy, England and the United States.

COFFEE: Beans carries 30 coffee varietals and blends, all roasted on the premises. Every day, there's a flavored, an unflavored and a decaf brew, served in handsome 12-ounce pottery mugs. Beans serves classic espresso drinks, nothing trendy. For tea aficionados, there is an impressive selection of loose-leaf teas, available by the pot or the pound, including rarities such as Hao-ya "B" Keemun, a China black tea, and Pan-Long-Ying Hao, a Zhejian green tea.

FOOD: The in-store bakery turns out scones (chocolate chunk, low-fat raisin, corn), muffins, Danish, croissants and a luscious caramel walnut bar. The lunch menu includes soups (try the spicy vegetable), sandwiches, salads, focaccia and "Beanzza"—pizza with a French-bread crust. Beans also carries about 15 varieties of fresh-baked breads, supplied by a local baker. The garlic-Parmesan-bacon loaf is outrageously good.

CLIENTELE: This is a neighborhood hangout populated by professionals, students from Boston College and Boston University, and families.

Orange Rum Raisin Bread Pudding
Beans, Boston, Massachusetts

9 eggs
3/4 cups sugar
2 1/4 cups milk
2 1/4 cups heavy cream
3/4 cup raisins
1/4 cup rum
1 teaspoon cinnamon
zest and juice of 1 orange
1 teaspoon vanilla extract
5 to 6 cups croissants cut into cubes (you can use plain, chocolate or fruit-filled croissants or sticky buns.)

1. Preheat oven to 350°F.
2. Mix eggs and sugar until thick and lemon colored in a large bowl.
3. Add milk, cream, rum, cinnamon, orange zest and juice, raisins and vanilla to egg mixture.
4. Add croissant cubes to egg mixture and toss until they're well coated. Let the mixture sit for one hour so that liquid has a chance to be absorbed.
5. Pour into a large, low baking dish and bake for 45 minutes until a knife inserted in the middle comes out clean.

At Cybersmith, a coffeehouse/computer store in Cambridge, Massachusetts, you can log on to one of 48 computers and test-drive the latest multimedia titles, virtual reality, video games, and the Internet. You can get food and coffee by clicking on Smitty's On-Line Cafe and placing your order on-line.

COFFEE CANTATA BISTRO & BEANS

605 Centre Street
Jamaica Plain, Massachusetts 02130 • (617) 522-2223
OPEN 7:30 A.M. TO 7 P.M. MONDAY;
7:30 A.M. TO 10 P.M. TUESDAY TO FRIDAY;
8:30 A.M. TO 10 P.M. SATURDAY; 9 A.M. TO 6 P.M. SUNDAY.

During the day, this cozy coffeehouse is a quiet place to relax or have a conversation, but at night it changes gear and becomes a bistro serving excellent food. The interior is simply lovely: rich, nectarine color-washed walls and mahogany wainscoting, a deep cranberry-colored ceiling, antique wood tables, chairs and barstools, and an old mosaic tile floor salvaged from the pharmacy that originally occupied the turn-of-the-century building. It's an intimate space, with seating for only 19 and an open kitchen where you can watch as your meal is prepared. Someone will greet you at the door, seat you and take your order, but feel free to order just a cup of coffee, even during the dinner rush—Cantata remains at heart a coffeehouse, not a restaurant.

COFFEE: Schapira Coffee and Tea, a New York roaster, supplies the coffee, including the Cantata house blend. The excellent cappuccino and caffe latte are made with a high ratio of espresso to milk.

FOOD: Co-owner Cynthia Bell makes all the baked goods on the premises, including sour cream streusel coffee cake, chocolate chip hazelnut biscotti, and cranberry-banana bread. Breakfast (mainly frittatas) is served daily, and on weekends the menu is expanded to include French toast, blintzes, and a smoked salmon platter. Lunch features sandwiches, pizzettas on herbed focaccia, and salads. At night, a bistro menu of pasta, ravioli and fish or meat specials is available. Finally, for dessert, try the sinfully rich Queen of Sheba chocolate hazelnut torte.

CLIENTELE: Cantata is a neighborhood haunt for professionals and artists who live in Jamaica Plain, a culturally and racially tolerant neighborhood just a 15-minute tolley ride from Boston's Back Bay.

Sour Cream Streusel Coffee Cake
Coffee Cantata Bistro & Beans, Jamaica Plain, Massachusetts

For streusel:

1/3 cup firmly packed light brown sugar
2 tablespoons white sugar
1 cup walnuts (shelled)
1 1/2 teaspoons cinnamon
1/2 cup flour
4 tablespoons butter at room temperature
1/2 teaspoon vanilla extract

For batter:

4 large egg yolks
2/3 cup sour cream
1 1/2 teaspoon vanilla extract
2 cups flour
1 cup sugar
1/2 teaspoon baking powder
1/2 teaspoon baking soda
1/4 teaspoon salt
12 tablespoons butter at room temperature

To make streusel filling and topping:

1. Filling: Combine sugars, nuts and cinnamon in food processor fitted with a metal blade and pulse until the nuts are coarsely chopped. Set aside 3/4 cups of streusel to be used as filling in the coffee cake.
2. Topping: Add flour, butter and vanilla to remaining mixture and pulse to form a coarse, crumbly topping for the cake.

To make batter:

1. Preheat oven to 350°F. Grease a 9-inch springform pan.
2. Mix together the yolks, vanilla and 3 tablespoons of the sour cream in a small bowl. Set aside.
3. In a large mixing bowl beat the butter until soft and creamy.
4. In a small bowl, mix together the flour, sugar, baking powder, baking soda and salt, then add this mixture and rest of the sour cream to the butter. Mix at low speed until the dry ingredients are moistened. Then beat at medium speed for 90 seconds.
5. Add the egg mixture, a little bit at a time, to the butter mixture, beating for 20 seconds after each addition.
6. Pour 1/2 of the batter into the prepared springform pan, spreading it out with a spatula so that it evenly covers the bottom of the pan. Sprinkle the filling on top, then cover with the remaining batter. Sprinkle the top with the streusel topping.
7. Bake 50 to 60 minutes until cake tester comes out clean. Cool before removing from pan.

PANINI

406 Washington Street
Somerville, Massachusetts 02143 • (617) 666-2770
OPEN 7 A.M. TO 8 P.M. MONDAY TO SATURDAY;
8 A.M. TO 5 P.M. SUNDAY.

This friendly bakery-cafe, open since 1990, attracts a loyal following of Harvard professors and local celebrities, including Julia Child and famed attorney Alan Dershowitz. Located just a few blocks from Harvard Square in a lovely 19th Century New England clapboard building, Panini has a well-deserved reputation for turning out the best breads and pastries in Boston. (Co-founder Debbie Merriam is also the chef at Olives, a highly regarded Boston restaurant.) The small interior is equally divided between the bakery and the cafe, with seating for only 26. Beneath the old tin ceiling sits a marble, glass and brass pharmacy case stocked with scones and other goodies, and a department store glove case filled with squares of freshly baked apple tart. Along the back wall, cookie jars and old baker's implements line the shelves for decoration.

COFFEE: Panini serves a dark roast from New York's Schapira Coffee and Tea. The espresso drink menu is simple and basic—no flavor shots, for example.

FOOD: The on-site bakery produces freshly baked goods seven days a week, including marvelous buttermilk scones (try the blackberry-ginger version), muffins, big, gooey Danish, and wonderful biscotti laden with almonds. You'll also find marvelous breads: white, sourdough, whole-wheat walnut, potato, country Italian, olive round and focaccia. For lunch, the cafe serves up sandwiches (roasted eggplant, ricotta and pesto is a favorite) and squares of delicious pizza topped with roasted garlic, ricotta and tomato, or potato, pesto and Parmesan.

CLIENTELE: Panini gets them all: Harvard Square weirdos and law school professors, working joes, poets, artists, and foodies.

DILWORTH COFFEEHOUSE

1235 East Boulevard
Charlotte, North Carolina 28203 • (704) 358-8003
OPEN 7:30 A.M. TO 11 P.M. SUNDAY TO THURSDAY;
7:30 A.M. TO MIDNIGHT FRIDAY AND SATURDAY.

Many residents of this Southern city got their first taste of quality coffee when Dilworth Coffeehouse opened in 1989 as a cafe-roaster. Located in the lively Dilworth neighborhood near downtown, this antiques-filled cafe no longer roasts on site (the roasting operation has moved to a larger location across town), but patrons still come for the excellent brew and homey atmosphere. The cafe, housed in a strip mall, has lots of windows, fans suspended from a high ceiling, and a mirrored wall that reflects the image of brass bins filled with coffee beans. Place your order at a 90-year-old oak counter that was salvaged from a country general store; your coffee will be served in a throwaway paper cup. You can sit at a marble-topped table or on a church pew, but the most sought-after seat is at an antique carpenter's table with six stools.

COFFEE: Dilworth roasts all its coffees. It offers five brews daily and basic espresso and iced coffee drinks. The house blend is the big seller.

FOOD: Everything is made off the premises by local bakers. There are bagels, muffins, pound cake and biscotti in the morning and gourmet desserts—cheesecake, Italian rum cake, carrot cake—in the afternoons and evenings.

CLIENTELE: Local business people, lawyers, architects and doctors from nearby Carolinas Medical Center come for their morning fix.

According to a 1989 University of London study, the caffeine in a cup of coffee can increase by 25 percent the number of calories your body burns from a small meal.

JEREMIAH'S COFFEE & TEA COMPANY

1408-BB East Boulevard
Charlotte, North Carolina 28203 • (704) 377-1680
OPEN 6:30 A.M. TO 9:30 P.M. MONDAY TO FRIDAY; 7 A.M. TO 9:30 P.M. SATURDAY AND SUNDAY

With its pale yellow faux-finished walls and low-voltage lighting, this coffeeshop exudes an air of elegant simplicity. Order your brew at the front counter, shaped like opposing coffee cups, then grab a stool and a nearby newspaper. There's usually soft music—jazz, classical or new Age—playing in the background. The crowd here is largely a commuter bunch who grab their coffee and go, so you may have the place all to yourself.

COFFEE: A menu board behind the counter lists the coffees and bulk beans. Jeremiah's carries a full line of espresso drinks (no flavored coffees, though). But the big draw here is regular coffee. Choose from 14 varieties and you'll get a fresh-made 16-ounce press pot for only a buck. There's also an extensive selection of teas: green, black, oolong and herbal. During the summer the iced coffees and teas are a big hit in steamy Charlotte.

FOOD: The coffee's the thing here, so don't come with a big appetite. you can order a baguette and butter, or one of the featured pastries of the day, all made off the premises.

CLIENTELE: Jeremiah's does 80 percent of its business before 11 a.m., selling road coffees to local bankers and workers at nearby Duke Power. In the afternoon, the crowd is more laid back, including local waiters just off from the lunch shift.

AURORA COFFEE

1205 17th Street
Miami Beach, Florida 33139 • (305) 534-1744
OPEN 6:30 A.M. TO 8 P.M. SUNDAY TO THURSDAY;
6:30 A.M. TO 10 P.M. FRIDAY AND SATURDAY.

Housed in the bottom floor of what used to be a hotel and is now an apartment building, Aurora is more espresso bar than coffeehouse—the goal at this up-tempo cafe is to get people in and out in a hurry. The bayside shop is narrow, with white and grey walls and a black ceiling that jut off at odd angles. Seating inside is limited; there's a bar with eight stools, but no tables or chairs. Order your coffee at the counter and it will be served to you in a paper cup unless you specify otherwise. If you intend to linger, go out back to the courtyard and find yourself a seat at one of the concrete patio tables, where the staff sometimes throw barbecues, complete with live music, for the patrons.

COFFEE: The company roasts its own coffee at its Atlanta headquarters. There's a house blend plus a brew of the day. In addition to the basic espresso drinks, there's something called the Shot in the Dark: drip coffee served with a shot of espresso.

FOOD: Just the coffeehouse basics: muffins, croissants and bagels, all from outside vendors.

CLIENTELE: In the morning, local business people on their way downtown stop in for coffee to go. In the late afternoon, employees from the area's many restaurants and bars fuel up before going to work. The place also gets dancers from the Miami City Ballet, which rehearses at a studio around the corner, and musicians with the New World Symphony, who perform nearby.

The morning cup of coffee has an exhilaration about it which the cheering influence of the afternoon or evening cup of tea cannot be expected to reproduce.

—Oliver Wendell Holmes, Sr., *Over the Teacups*

GERTRUDE'S

826 Lincoln Road Mall
Miami Beach, Florida 33139 • (305) 538-6929
OPEN NOON TO MIDNIGHT DAILY.

Named after Lost Generation author Gertrude Stein, this atmospheric cafe in Miami Beach's chic Art Deco District has a devoted following of artists and local residents. Located in a trendy pedestrian mall, Gertrude's is a quietly pleasant place to read or study. With its big windows, high ceiling and ceiling fans, it has an airy charm. At night, candlelight gives it a more sophisticated glow. One long wall is adorned with a mural of Stein and Alice B. Toklas; the others feature a changing exhibit of local artists' work. The coffee here is lovingly prepared to order, and some of the pastries are flown in from Milan. But the real draw here is the friendly, experienced staff, who treat customers like family.

COFFEE: The delicious brewed coffee, which is roasted using a mineral water process, is made to order and served in press pots. The flavored cappuccino drinks are named after Stein and her pals. There's the Gertrude cappuccino (flavored with hazelnut and creme de cacao), the Alice (almond and coconut), and the Missy (chocolate mint). Italian cream sodas are also available.

FOOD: Gertrude's carries an astounding array of fat-free muffins, cakes, cookies and cheesecakes, all made off the premises. The cafe also imports tiramisu, berry tarts and other sweets from Bindi of Milan. For lunch and dinner, you can order typical coffeehouse fare: soups, salads and deli-style sandwiches.

CLIENTELE: Gertrude's is an adjunct campus for Florida International University students. There's also plenty of local business owners, folks from the surrounding suburbs, and European tourists.

NEWS CAFE

800 Ocean Drive
Miami Beach, Florida 33139 • (305) 531-0392
OPEN 24 HOURS A DAY.

In hot Miami, this Art Deco District hangout is the epitome of cool. Models, fashion industry moguls, and celebrities from the sports and entertainment worlds (do the names Madonna and Stallone mean anything to you?) come here to buy their foreign magazines and wallow in the place's overarching European hipness. Co-owner Mark Soyka, an Israeli native who lived in New York for 20 years before migrating south, planned News Cafe as an American version of a European news kiosk: a place where one could buy the morning paper along with coffee and a croissant. But it turned into something even greater: a must-be place to see and be seen, to cruise and be cruised. Girl and boy watching here is a favorite activity. Others come for the food (an extensive menu is available 24 hours a day) or just to hang out on the enormous patio (it seats 200) and enjoy the sight of palm trees and blue ocean. On unbearably muggy days, patrons can duck inside, where there are terrazzo floors, dark wood bars and tropical wood fans. The staff, who take your order at the table, encourage patrons to linger as long as they like.

COFFEE: You won't find an endless selection of coffees, merely the basics (espresso, cappuccino, etc.), plus American coffee, Cuban coffee and cafe con leche. News Cafe also has a full licensed bar.

FOOD: The menu, which is served all day long, includes traditional breakfast fare (eggs, bagels and lox, pastries), plus a laundry list of lunch and dinner items: burgers, salads, sandwiches, soups, pastas and steaks. For dessert, you'll find tiramisu, lemon pound cake, Key lime pie, and chocolate fondue.

CLIENTELE: The crowd is at least 50 percent European and includes models and fashion magazine folk doing photo shoots on the beach just across the street, and Hollywood types who flock to Miami's trendy South Beach. Club goers and transvestites in full plumage come out at night.

9

110 St. Marks Place
New York , New York 10009 • (212) 982-7129
OPEN 10 A.M. TO 1 A.M. MONDAY TO THURSDAY; 10 A.M. TO 2 A.M. FRIDAY AND SATURDAY; 10 A.M. TO MIDNIGHT SUNDAY.

Co-owners June LaMarca and Mollie Parks consulted with a numerologist to come up with the name for this East Village coffeehouse. LaMarca, a former caterer, was inspired to open this West Coast-style cafe after a driving trip from San Francisco to Seattle. The interior has a dramatic feel, with a purple ceiling that bleeds into blue walls, strikingly lit brickwork and hand-painted chairs and tables created by theatrical designers Jason Boyd and Derek Stenborg. The American coffee comes to the table in French press pots from Bodum. The staff run the gamut from pierced and dyed to primped and poofed, making this a favorite spot with hip teenagers and business people.

COFFEE: There's an organic house coffee and four blends that change daily from Longo Coffee & Tea, a Brooklyn roaster. The Ciccheli espresso and Entner-Stuart syrups are from Eurobar, and the authentic Chinese teas are from Ten-Ren's Tea House.

FOOD: For breakfast, there are excellent bagels from an outside supplier. A full brunch menu is served seven days a week and includes pain perdu (New Orleans style French toast), mozzarella, tomato and basil omelette, vegan tofu scramble and LaMarca's amazing granola. For dessert, the kitchen turns out tiramisu, maple brulee and peanut butter pie.

CLIENTELE: Not-so-starving local artists come in to eat the hearty breakfasts, which are served daily until 4 p.m. On the weekends, 9 gets heavy commuter traffic from uptown and the outer buroughs.

Peanut Butter Pie
9, New York

For crust:

2 cups unsalted peanuts, coarsely chopped
1/2 cup semisweet chocolate mini chips
1/4 cup sugar
1/3 cup butter, melted

For filling:

8 ounces cream cheese, softened
1/2 cup creamy peanut butter
3/4 cup confectioner's sugar
1/2 cup milk
1 cup heavy cream, whipped to stiff peaks
chocolate chips or chocolate shavings for garnish

To make crust:

1. Mix the ingredients together and press the mixture into a 9-inch pie pan. Freeze while preparing the filling.

To make fillng:

1. Beat together cream cheese and peanut butter. Add sugar and mix thoroughly. Add enough milk to make the mixture smooth without thinning it.
2. Fold whipped cream into peanut butter mixture and mix thoroughly.
3. Fill pie crust with peanut butter mixture, cover and freeze for at least 6 hours.
4. To serve, let pie defrost in the refrigerator for 1 to 2 hours. Garnish with chocolate chips or shavings.

The stars of NBC's Frasier *and* Seinfeld *drink Starbucks coffee on the set. Jerry Seinfeld dilutes his with Lactaid milk.*

ESPRESSO MADISON

33 East 68th Street
New York, New York 10021 • (212) 988-7444
OPEN 8 A.M. TO 6:30 P.M. MONDAY TO SATURDAY;
CLOSED SUNDAY.

This Italian espresso bar on Manhattan's Upper East Side is as authentic as the cafes you find on every street corner in Milan. It's a gathering place for Italian ex-patriates who live and work in the neighborhood. (Within one block is the Italian consulate, the Italian Cultural Center, and the retail shops of designers Giorgio Armani, Valentino and Versace.) Espresso Madison, which shares an elegant stone building on the corner of Madison and 68th with the Max Mara boutique, is a tiny mahogany jewelbox of a bar, with only two seats and standing room for about 25. Patrons crowd in at lunchtime to eat exquisite panini sandwiches and drink the Lavazza coffee or if they're in a celebratory mood, a glass of Veuve Cliquot Champagne, served by waiters in blue shirts, navy ties, and classic sommelier aprons that fall to the floor.

COFFEE: The staff pulls authentic "short" espressos and cappuccinos just like in a Milanese coffee bar, and the espresso machines are lovingly cleaned and maintained to ensure quality. In addition to the coffee and strong Dutch hot chocolate, there's fresh, blood-orange juice, San Pellegrino sodas, Italian wines and beers, and French Champagne.

FOOD: For breakfast you'll find European pastries such as croissants, brioche, scones and hard rolls. The European-style sandwiches, served on Italian country bread, include mozzarella, tomato and basil, grilled lemon chicken, and eggplant and mozzarella. For dessert there's an exquisite berry tart.

CLIENTELE: A good 98 percent of the patrons here are European, and include well-dressed, well-spoken people from the fashion, cultural and diplomtic realms. Italian fashion designers and magazine editors drop by when they're in town.

EUREKA JOE

168 Fifth Avenue

New York, New York 10010 • (212) 741-7500

OPEN 7 A.M. TO 9 P.M. MONDAY TO FRIDAY;
9 A.M. TO 9 P.M. SATURDAY; 10 A.M. TO 6 P.M. SUNDAY.

Plop yourself down on a velvet-covered sofa in this hypertrendy cafe in Manhattan's Flatiron District and prepare to meet the New Yorker of your dreams. Since its opening in 1993, Eureka Joe has been the place for hip young things to come and flirt. Chances are that fabulous-looking creature at the next table is a model or a photographer, or maybe a rising young executive with a major record label. Even the waiters here (most of them aspiring models and actors) are great looking. The huge, inviting space has a hotel-lobby ambience, with scattered sofas and armchairs, and a flattering pinkish lighting that gives everyone an instant tan. Striking metal sculptures by Soho artist Monica Banks line the walls, and there's a red mahogany counter and stools where you can sit and people watch. On Monday nights a palm reader reads fortunes for free.

COFFEE: New Jersey roaster Oren Bloostein created the house coffee, a rich, full-bodied Guatemalan Coban. The house special is the New York-to-Los Angeles Red Eye, a high-octane mix of the house coffee with a shot of espresso. You can also order organic juices, fresh cranberry lemonade, and Joe's Protein Drink, made with TwinLab protein powder.

FOOD: The pastries, supplied by top New York bakers, include chocolate mousse cake, creamy Key lime squares, jam-filled walnut scones, and organic doughnuts that disappear as soon as they arrive. Co-owner David Pearlberg runs the kitchen, which serves high-quality soups, salads and sandwiches, such as grilled chicken with black olive mayonnaise on onion focaccia, and goat cheese with sun-dried tomatoes on a whole-wheat baguette. The menu changes daily.

CLIENTELE: During the week, it's a fashionable crowd: models on go-sees with photographers, journalists conducting interviews over coffee with celebrities, and publishing and recording executives meeting for lunch. The area's groovy boutiques bring in a lot of fashionable shoppers. On

Saturdays and Sundays, a different crowd prevails: Manhattanites from the Upper East and West Sides slumming downtown, and the suburbs' dreaded bridge and tunnel set come for an authentic New York experience.

CLAUDIA FIGALLO, 24, aspiring "expressive therapist," Brooklyn:

A native of Venezuela, Figallo works temporarily at a children's magazine, but plans to return to college for her master's degree in expressive therapy, a form of psychological therapy using play-acting, masks, puppets and dance to bring out feelings. Her daily cafe visit gives her a chance to relax, read and write short stories, and also provides a convenient place to meet her friends after work before going out on the town.

FAVORITE DRINK: It changes often. "I like iced coffees. Flavored au laits. Mocha latte. Right now, I'm having a cinnamon cafe au lait, iced. It's filling."

PER DIEM: Two cups. More than that is just too much.

FAVORITE CAFE: Eureka Joe, near her workplace.

ON EUREKA JOE'S REPUTATION AS A PLACE TO MEET SOMEONE INTERESTING: "Oh, gee, I haven't been that lucky. I guess it is a good place for eyes to meet, but I'm too focused on what I'm reading or writing." She hangs out in the back where there are fewer people.

WHAT THE CAFE MEANS TO HER: "It's not so much the coffee, but the break it gives me. It's therapeutic. If I've been running around all day, it relaxes me enough to get back in focus with myself."

JOE BAR

250 West 91st Street (on Broadway)
New York, New York 10024 • (212) 787-3684
OPEN 7 A.M. TO 9 P.M. MONDAY TO THURSDAY;
7 A.M. TO 11 P.M. FRIDAY; 8 A.M. TO 11 P.M. SATURDAY;
8 A.M. TO 9 P.M. SUNDAY

The residents of this artsy neighborhood known as the Upper Upper West Side have embraced this tiny coffee bar and made it their own. Located on the corner of 91st and Broadway, it's got a mid-tech look that's neither cold and sterile nor frou-frou, with an exposed brick wall, halogen pendant lamps, and a big curved wood bar where friendly staffers greet patrons by name. There's also window seating where customers can hang out, write in their journals and watch the world go by. Young matrons perch on mesh-seated stools at bar-height tables and gossip as their toddlers romp undisturbed at their feet. At night, the staff lights candles on the counter and tabletops for a warm, cozy glow.

COFFEE: The coffee comes from a local roaster and is served in paper cups, because there are no dishwashing facilities on the premises. The house specialty, the Triple Whammy, is a hazelnut and chocolate flavored cappuccino. Cocoa and hot cider are also available.

FOOD: You'll find the usual coffeehouse baked goods, soups and sandwiches, all made by offsite suppliers.

CLIENTELE: The regulars include photographers, film directors, actors, writers, artists and musicians who live in the neighborhood.

The characters on Friends, *an NBC hit television show, meet to bicker and gossip at a Manhattan cafe called Central Perk.*

KAFFEEHAUS

131 8th Avenue
New York, New York 10011 • (212) 229-9702
OPEN 11:30 A.M. TO 1 A.M. MONDAY TO THURSDAY;
11 A.M. TO 1 A.M. FRIDAY AND SATURDAY;
11 A.M. TO MIDNIGHT SUNDAY.

From the waltzes playing in the background to the authentic schlag that accompanies the coffee and pastries, Kaffeehaus is a true Viennese cafe. Located in the Chelsea district between 16th and 17th streets, it is a feast for the eyes, with marble-topped tables, maroon cut-velvet banquettes, and a dramatic copper-topped bar. At night the yellow-walled room is cozy and romantic, especially in winter, when the velvet draperies at the front door are drawn to keep out the chilly New York wind. While the ambience is turn-of-the-century Vienna, the crowd is anything but stuffy: it's heavy on models, artists and stylish young Europeans. During non-peak hours you can sit and sip a coffee (served Viennese style on a metal tray along with a tiny glass of palate-cleansing water), but at lunch and dinner the tables are reserved for serious dining. The extensive menu features Austrian specialties such astafelspitz (braised beef), along with European-style pastries such as strudels and tortes, served by solicitous waiters clad in black pants, starched white shirts and long white aprons. In summer there's seating on the sidewalk out front, where French doors open up to the street.

COFFEE: Kaffeehaus serves a number of Austrian coffee drinks, including Melange (the Viennese version of cappuccino, made with two shots of espresso), Einspenner (a long double espresso served with whipped cream), and Brauner (a short double espresso, served with schlag, or heavy cream, on the side). A house specialty is Cafe Schokolade, a cappuccino blended with hot chocolate. Kaffeehaus uses top-of-the-line Illycaffe, and espresso here is made very short, in the European style, unless otherwise requested. The cafe also carries a fine selection of wines and liqueurs.

FOOD: Austrian dishes dominate the lunch and dinner menus. For lunch, start with the organic field salad with roasted pumpkin seed oil vinaigrette, served with or without warm goat cheese, and the oven-roasted lamb sausage with spaghetti squash and white bean goulash. Main courses include Wiener schnitzel and free-range egg omelette. The dinner menu includes mouth-watering dishes such as smoked salmon tartare on crisp rosti potatoes with salmon roe and field greens; pan-roasted striped bass with poppyseed spatzle and fried leeks; and rib-eye steak with port wine sauce. The dessert case features hand-pulled strudel, Linzer torte, and mocha dacquoise, among other treats. Prices here are surprisingly gentle by Manhattan standards.

CLIENTELE: The crowd is truly eclectic: Uptown sophisticates and Downtown club crawlers, members of the International set, and beautiful people of both sexes.

In a popular college drinking game, participants watching the TV show Frasier *must take a drink every time Niles Crane dusts off his chair in Cafe Nervosa.*

MAKAM'S KITCHEN

2401 Lombard Street
Philadelphia, Pennsylvania 19146
(215) 546-8832
OPEN 10 A.M. TO 10 P.M DAILY.

Part coffeehouse, part restaurant, this offbeat cafe is a popular hangout for Philadelphia's international contingent. Located halfway between Center City and the University of Pennsylvania in a dumpy-looking corner building, it's got a style all its own: doors and window frames painted different colors, an orange kitchen, a big silk scarf hanging from the ceiling, and an Indian ganesh standing watch over the customers. Four shelves hold an assortment of old books and games—Scrabble, Pictionary, dominoes and Monopoly—for patrons to amuse themselves with. Ten small tables are covered with red tablecloths. The space is so intimate that every conversation can be overheard, so don't come here if you like to be anonymous.

COFFEE: Makam's serves coffee, espresso and Greek coffee from New Harmony, a local roaster.

FOOD: Owner Lori Marks, a vegetarian, does all the cooking. The menu includes soup (perhaps lentil feta or black bean and orange), vegetable curries and stews, and Greek spanakopita (spinach pie). There's also an assortment of sandwiches, including the Ananda—hummus, provolone, radishes, onions and cucumbers on pumpernickel—and the Lori bagel—cream cheese, capers, onion and tomato on a toasted bagel.

CLIENTELE: Artists, grad students from Penn, history and psych majors from Temple University, and local Greeks, Spaniards and Italians.

RHINO COFFEE CO. ROASTERY & CAFE

212 South Street
Philadelphia, Pennsylvania 19147 • (215) 923-2630
OPEN 7:30 A.M. TO MIDNIGHT MONDAY TO THURSDAY;
7:30 TO 1 A.M. FRIDAY ; 9 A.M. TO 1 A.M. SATURDAY;
9 A.M. TO MIDNIGHT SUNDAY.

Rhino, which opened in 1993, was the first coffeehouse to appear on Philly's trendy South Street. A long, narrow space located in an old brickfront building, it is a relaxed place with a loyal clientele and experienced staff who know their coffee. The large front window lets in lots of natural light, and classical and jazz music play softly in the background. Owner Anders Divack, trained as a restaurant chef, has thrown himself into the coffee business; he roasts his own in the store. Rhino seats about 30 in a small dining area and at the bar.

COFFEE: Rhino offers a varietal that changes daily. There's also the signature Rhinoblast (a gelato-based milkshake with a double shot of espresso), the frozen espresso smoothie, and the white chocolate mocha.

FOOD: At the counter you can purchase pastries from local suppliers.

CLIENTELE: Customers range from affluent residents of nearby Queen Village and Society Hill, business people on their way to work, and college kids. People with time on their hands sit and play chess or checkers.

MONIQUE RIGLING, 31, massage therapist, Philadelphia:

Rigling, who is single, has no problem going where she wants to go, and doing what she wants to do alone. She's traveled solo in Europe and Mexico and goes to movies, plays, museums and concerts alone. "I'd rather be alone than with someone just for the sake of not being alone." She rarely goes to bars: "Guys say the weirdest things to me in bars."

FAVORITE DRINK: Black coffee, Ethiopian roast. French roast is too heavy.

PER DIEM: One cup in the morning, and some decaf in the afternoon.

FAVORITE CAFE: Right now, it's Rhino. "It's close to home," she says, eating a non-fat muffin and reading the *New York Times* Sunday magazine and book review. Operatic music plays in the background. "Today's my day off. I'll be here maybe three hours." But she likes to check out new cafes. "Depends on what mood I'm in."

PHILOSOPHY: Living in Europe in the mid-1980s, she appreciated how many people there worked just enough to enjoy life. "That's my aim," she says. A college anthropology major, she drifted through "what must have been 20 bad jobs" before finding something in which she can be her own boss. "Doing massage therapy affords me the time to read, relax, do artwork, be with friends."

THE BEEHIVE COFFEEHOUSE AND DESSERTERY

1327 East Carson Street
Pittsburgh, Pennsylvania 15203 • (412) 488-4483
OPEN 8:30 A.M. TO 1 A.M. SUNDAY TO THURSDAY; 8:30 A.M. TO 3 A.M. FRIDAY AND SATURDAY.

Pittsburgh's first official coffeehouse (it opened in 1991), the Beehive gained a measure of national notoriety when it was touted in *Details* and *Entertainment Weekly* as one of the coolest spots in town. Located in Pittsburgh's Southside, a hip artists' neighborhood near downtown, the Beehive has a '60s coffeehouse 'tude that attracts bikers, bohos, and other counterculture folk. The small corner shop has big windows, wood floors, the classic mismatched furniture, and a 13-foot-high ceiling painted with clouds. Head for the service counter, where a laid-back employee will pour you a cup of superior coffee, served in a mug from Goodwill. For fun, check out Beehive's other location, a coffeehouse/movie theater about a mile away (at 3807 Forbes Avenue, (412) 683-4483) that shows first-run art films and cult classics.

COFFEE: The Beehive gets its coffee from a New York roaster that it refuses to name. It serves a house blend and standard espresso drinks, as well as 16 coffee blends made and served in French press pots.

FOOD: The food is prepared off the premises and includes muffins, scones and croissants, cakes, and prepackaged health foods such as hummus and baba ganoush.

CLIENTELE: Coffee addicts, bikers, musicians, artists and professors all call the Beehive home.

SIP CAFE

238 Shady Avenue
Pittsburgh, Pennsylvania 15206 • (412) 361-4478
OPEN 8 A.M. TO MIDNIGHT MONDAY TO FRIDAY;
10 A.M. TO MIDNIGHT SATURDAY AND SUNDAY.

Don't let the bland facade of Sip Cafe fool you; inside is Pittsburgh's hippest coffeehouse. Located in the East End, it takes up the ground floor of an old Victorian row house that years ago was stripped of all its charm and ornamentation during a rehab. But owner Brian Glover has compensated by turning the old parlour into a delightful space, with a Victorian rug over pine floors and sponge-painted walls in reds, greens and blues combined to create a deep, textured finish. Overhead hang lightbulbs with muslin shades hand-painted with Gorey-esque figures by an artist friend, and the striking tables are made of steel pipe topped with concrete or marble slabs. But the room's focus is an enormous window, draped with a fabric swag, that overlooks the sidewalk and brick patio out front, where patrons can sit in the summer months.

COFFEE: The coffee comes from Rhino Coffee Co. in Philadelphia, which makes the "Zen blend" house coffee from Ethiopian, Sumatran and French roast beans. Refills are free. The concept here is to be as traditional and simple as possible, so the espresso drinks are just the basics—no flavorings or syrups. The cafe mocha is made by pouring hot espresso over chopped Belgian chocolate; Sip Cafe also makes a white chocolate mocha with chopped white chocolate.

FOOD: There's no kitchen to speak of here, so the food is prepared off the premises. Breakfast includes bagels, croissants and scones; for lunch, there's soup (lentil or Moroccan vegetable) and Middle Eastern and Moroccan vegetarian dishes.

CLIENTELE: The crowd is gay and straight and includes club kids, neighborhood writers and artists, and college professors from Carnegie Mellon and the University of Pittsburgh. Foreign exchange students come here to smoke.

THE STRIP BAR

1814 Penn Avenue
Pittsburgh, Pennsylvania 15222 • (412) 471-1043
OPEN 8 A.M. TO MIDNIGHT SUNDAY TO THURSDAY;
8 A.M. TO 4 A.M. FRIDAY AND SATURDAY.

This coffeehouse in the Strip District was opened in 1994 by a former Coloradan looking to bring a bit of the West Coast to Pittsburgh. Whimsy abounds, with purple walls painted with lavender clouds, an enormous chalkboard where customers can express themselves, and old, rustic window frames suspended from the ceiling. For fun, there's a huge moose sculpture, made by a local artist from old metal and burlap sacks, that patrons can ride. The seating area is cozy and private, with mismatched marble-topped tables and chairs, and old sofas where you can sink down and relax. When the place is crowded, you can stand at the copper-topped bar and drink coffee from enormous ceramic cups, served up by great-looking employees.

COFFEE: The coffee, from California roaster F. Gavina & Sons, includes two brews that change daily. The espresso specials change as well; try the Sledgehammer, made with four shots of espresso, half and half, and sugar.

FOOD: Everything's made off the premises, including chocolate chip scones, apple cinnamon muffins, and individual cinnamon pecan coffee cakes. There's also soup, pasta salad, gourmet sandwiches and pizzas. For dessert, try the chocolate mousse cake or the peanut butter bottom pie.

CLIENTELE: A group of Italian men hang out here during the day, talking loudly and playing cards. At night, the crowd is a diverese collection of students and locals.

COFFEE EXCHANGE

207 Wickenden Street
Providence, Rhode Island 02903 • (401) 273-1198
OPEN 6 :30 A.M. TO 11 P.M. DAILY.

The Coffee Exchange, founded in 1984 by brothers Charles and Bill Fishbein, is Providence's quintessential coffeehouse, a laid-back place where you can park yourself all day long and no one will bother you. It started out as a retail store selling coffee beans and paraphernalia. Later, the Fishbeins added a few tables and chairs. Eventually, it grew so popular they had to move to larger digs in a turn-of-the-century building across the street. Coffee Exchange is located in Fox Point, a Bohemian neighborhood where students from nearby Brown University, the Rhode Island School of Design, and Providence and Rhode Island colleges converge. The decor is haphazard: commercial pots and pans hanging from the ceiling, shelves displaying coffeemakers and grinders for sale, and walls plastered with Roommate Wanted notices, ads for local businesses and posters for upcoming cultural events. Coffee Exchange is always busy, especially in the evening.

COFFEE: Coffee is roasted on the premises in a back room. Every day, there's six brews to choose from: the house Naragansett blend, French roast, Mel's Private Stock (a special decaf blend), and a dark roast, a regular roast, and a decaf roast that change daily. Coffee Exchange serves a full range of espresso and flavored espresso drinks. The specialty is the Ambulance Chaser, also known as the Quad 911: four shots of espresso. ("No milk, no cream, no liability," says owner Charles Fishbein.)

FOOD: A long counter is piled high with homemade goodies—scones, muffins, brownies, biscotti, etc.—from a local baker. You'll also find a sweet, frosted Portuguese popover called a cavaca.

CLIENTELE: Preppies from Brown and counterculture types from RISD (Rhode Island School of Design), make this their home away from home. You'll also find business types in suits and ties, carrying laptops and cellular phones.

PASTICHE

92 Spruce Street
Providence, Rhode Island 02903 • (401) 861-5190
OPEN 8:30 A.M. TO 11 P.M. TUESDAY TO THURSDAY;
8:30 A.M. TO 11:30 P.M. FRIDAY AND SATURDAY;
10 A.M. TO 10 P.M. SUNDAY. CLOSED MONDAY.

This charming patisserie on Federal Hill, the Italian section of Providence, is a mecca for locals looking for fabulous coffee and baked goods. Started by husband-and-wife team Brandt Heckert and Eileen Collins as a wholesale bakery, Pastiche expanded into a small storefront on an out-of-the-way side street in the late '80s. The shop, housed in a 110-year-old clapboard building, combines historical quaintness with clean, modern lines. An art college pal of the owners designed the interior, with stained and pitted hardwood floors, glazed peach walls, and a giant mural of Tuscany. On cold nights, a fire roars in the fireplace. The generously supplied dessert case is the room's focus, bathed in dramatic light from overhead spots. The atmosphere here is bustling; with only 28 seats, the staff works fast to accommodate the constant stream of customers.

COFFEE: The excellent house coffee, a blend of Sumatran and French roast, comes from Ocean Roasters. In addition, you can order the pricey Cafe LaSemeuse, which is served in a French press pot.

FOOD: You'll find only desserts here—but what desserts! There's torta di cioccolata, a flourless chocolate torte with raspberry sauce, whipped cream and fresh raspberries. Other top sellers include mascarpone torte (a tiramisu-like pie), caramel-banana cream tart, and an all-American chocolate layer cake. There are cookies, including lemon squares, chocolate-walnut truffle cookies, and orange-almond crunch. And Pastiche serves daily specials: perhaps a fresh strawberry shortcake, or a warm blueberry cobbler with homemade ice cream that's big enough to share. For breakfast, you'll find muffins, scones, and a wonderfully chewy, crunchy almond biscotti. It goes without saying that everything is made on the premises.

CLIENTELE: Customers tend to be a bit older than college age: people looking for dessert after dinner at one of the area's Italian restaurants.

Apple Tart
Pastiche, Providence, Rhode Island

For tart shell:

1 1/2 cups all-purpose flour
2 tablespoons sugar
4 ounces cold unsalted butter
1 egg yolk
1 tablespoon cold water
pinch of salt

For filling:

4 large baking apples, peeled, cored and finely chopped
1/2 cup sugar
1 tablespoon cornstarch
1/2 teaspoon cinnamon
2 tablespoons unsalted butter
2 tablespoons water

For topping:

3 to 4 large baking apples, peeled, cored and thinly sliced
1/4 cup sugar
1 teaspoon cinnamon
apricot jam for glaze

To make tart shell:

1. Sift together the flour, sugar and salt in a large bowl.
2. Cut the butter into small pieces. Using a pastry cutter or your fingers cut the butter into the dry ingredients until mixture resembles coarse crumbs.
3. Stir in the yolk and water until the mixture just holds together.
4. Form the dough into a ball, flatten it slightly, then wrap and refrigerate for at least two hours.
5. On a lightly floured surface, roll out the dough into a 13-inch circle. Press the dough into an 11-inch tart pan. Place the pan in the freezer for an hour to keep the shell from shrinking during baking.
6. Line the shell with foil and pie weights or dried beans, then bake at 350°F for approximately 20 minutes until golden brown.

To make filling:

1. Mix the sugar, cornstarch and cinnamon in a small bowl.
2. Melt the butter in a large saucepan. Add the apples, water and dry ingredients. Bring to a low boil, stirring often, until the apples are soft and the cornstarch is clear.
3. Cool to room temperature.

To assemble:

1. Preheat oven to 350°F degrees.
2. Fill the prebaked tart shell with cooled apple mixture. Arrange sliced apples on top in a decorative pattern.
3. Mix the sugar and cinnamon, and sprinkle on top of the tart.
4. Bake for 45 minutes.
5. To make the glaze, heat the apricot jam and thin slightly with water. Brush the glaze onto the cooled tart.
6. Serve the tart at room temperature, or warm it slightly in the oven. Serve with good-quality vanilla ice cream or lightly sweetened whipped cream.

FIREHOOK BAKERY & COFFEEHOUSE

106 North Lee Street
Alexandria, Virginia 22314 • (703) 519-8020
OPEN 7 A.M. TO 6 P.M. MONDAY;
7 A.M. TO 8 P.M. TUESDAY TO SATURDAY;
8 A.M. TO 6 P.M. SUNDAY.

Located in the quaint Old Town section of Alexandria (an upscale suburb of Washington, D.C.), this inviting cafe is known for its fabulous European-style breads, which are baked on the premises in a brick wood-burning oven. Firehook (which takes its name from an Egyptian bread-making tool) shares a renovated warehouse building with an Italian deli and a party-goods store; with no walls to separate it from its neighbors, the place has an open market feel. Patrons pick up a tray and move through a cafeteria-style line, choosing items from the coffee and juice bars, the breakfast bar, and the baked goods area. Customers can watch as the staff chop herbs, grate cheese, and place loaves in the oven to bake. (The smell is heavenly.) There are tables and chairs in a common area shared with the deli, as well as a counter and barstools at the front window. But turnover here is brisk; it's more eat-and-run than hangout.

COFFEE: The coffee bar features free refills on the house blend and the flavored coffee of the week. It also offers a special espresso-based drink of the week at a reduced price. At the juice bar, you can watch as your juice (using whatever fruit's in season) is squeezed to order.

FOOD: Don't miss the breads, made from a natural sourdough starter, including a traditional French baguette, Swiss mountain bread, Italian focaccia, and green olive bread. Displayed on glass shelves, they are available by the slice or the loaf. Firehook is renowned for its French toast, made with its own day-old bread. You'll also find homemade scones, fresh fruit tarts, sinful chocolate raspberry truffle cake (sold whole and by the slice), and chocolate-espresso cookies. If you're looking for lunch or dinner, walk a few feet across the room to the Italian deli.

CLIENTELE: Firehook is a favorite with well-to-do Old Town residents, tourists, and folks from the District who come for the great bread. Hillary Clinton and First Kid Chelsea have come in for muffins.

KRAMERBOOKS & AFTERWORDS CAFE

1517 Connecticut Avenue N.W.
Washington, D.C. 20036 • (202) 387-1462
OPEN 7:30 A.M. TO 1 A.M. SUNDAY TO THURSDAY;
OPEN ALL DAY AND NIGHT FRIDAY AND SATURDAY.

Kramerbooks & Afterwords in Washington, D.C.'s trendy Dupont Circle neighborhood is as much a D.C. landmark as the White House or the Jefferson Memorial. Opened in 1976, it was D.C.'s first combination bookstore/cafe, and its popularity continues to grow. It's more than a coffeehouse, with a restaurant menu and a liquor license, but you can sit and drink just a coffee when no one's waiting for a table. There's seating for about 50 in the back of the bookstore, in the mezzanine above, and out back in the glass-enclosed solarium, which has an entrance on 19th Street. Waiters take your order in the dining area, but you can belly up to the espresso bar for a quick coffee. Make sure you browse the bookstacks; this is also one of the best bookstores in town.

COFFEE: In addition to a full bar, Kramerbooks & Afterwords offers high-quality coffee, fresh ground for each pot.

FOOD: There's a breakfast menu, plus a la carte muffins, bagels and biscotti. At lunch and dinner, chef Peter Barich provides interesting international fare, such as Thai jambalaya. Desserts are not for the faint of heart and include a marvelous chocolate-coconut sour cream cake and Kahlua walnut pie. Brunch is served Saturdays and Sundays.

CLIENTELE: Kramerbrooks & Afterwords attracts customers from all over the District, including businessmen, artists and the post-dinner crowds. Tourists also come, clutching guidebooks that tout this popular spot.

DON WILLIAMS, 62, retired chemical engineer, Washington, D.C.:

When Williams first saw a cafe-bookstore open in his neighborhood some 15 years ago, he thought: "What a dumb idea." Now, he drops by not once but three times a day. He has two cups at 7:30 a.m., another on a return trip at 11 a.m., and a couple more—decaffeinated this time—in the late afternoon.

FAVORITE DRINK: "My cup is just plain old American coffee, black."

PER DIEM: Five to six, all at his favorite hangout.

FAVORITE CAFE: Kramerbooks & Afterwords, a few blocks from his home. "I come for the social aspects." He specializes in talking politics (left liberal) and sports.

QUOTE: "I like to schmooze. I know all the employees, the owners and a dozen other regulars. This place is my home away from home."

A barista *works behind the bar of a coffeehouse, pouring shots of espresso and mixing up coffee drinks.*

POLITICS AND PROSE BOOKSTORE AND COFFEEHOUSE

5015 Connecticut Avenue N.W.
Washington, D.C. 20008 • (202) 364-1919
OPEN 8:30 A.M. TO 10:30 P.M. SUNDAY TO THURSDAY;
8:30 A.M. TO MIDNIGHT FRIDAY AND SATURDAY.

Located at the border of Washington and Chevy Chase, Maryland, this delightful coffeehouse shares space with a well-stocked bookstore, and the owners encourage patrons to move freely between the two. There are couches and easy chairs in the bilevel store, where you can sit with a coffee and browse your way through stacks of new, quality books. If you prefer, you can sit at a funky wood table in the cafe at the shop's rear, where you'll find good food, coffee served in hefty ceramic mugs and a selection of newspapers (the *Washington Post, New York Times* and *Wall Street Journal*) for the customers to read. The atmosphere is lively and comfortable. Help yourself to free refills from air pots on the counter; the friendly staff will happily steam up more milk for your latte.

COFFEE: Politics and Prose, which gets its coffee from local roasters Quartermaine and Roasters on the Hill, serves three brews that change daily and a full line of espresso and iced coffee drinks.

FOOD: The coffeehouse fare includes New York crumb cake, low-fat blueberry squares, poundcake, and muffins and scones, all made by local bakers. For lunch, there are soups, salads and sandwiches; favorites include a zucchini fritter sandwich, and the Popeye Special: sauteed spinach, mushrooms, onions and mozzarella on your choice of breads. The desserts change daily and might include tiramisu, cappuccino cake, lemon squares, Sacher torte or cream cheese brownies.

CLIENTELE: In the morning, business people and stroller moms come to read the paper in peace and quiet. Later in the day, there's a livelier and louder crowd of American University students and local residents.

THE POP STOP

1513 17th Street N.W.
Washington, D.C. 20036 • (202) 328-0880
OPEN 7:30 A.M. TO 2 A.M. SUNDAY TO THURSDAY;
7:30 A.M. TO 4 A.M. FRIDAY AND SATURDAY.

This is one of the busiest coffeehouses in Washington. Located in an old, three-story Victorian that once housed a Chinese laundromat, The Pop Stop is now a hangout for Dupont Circle denizens, particularly this neighborhood's large gay population. It's packed on Monday nights, when patrons gather to watch *Melrose Place* on TV. The decor is similarly kitschy: yard sale furniture and greenish-yellow walls painted with purple flowers. Entering the building, you'll find a rack of alternative newspapers and a bulletin board crammed with Roommate Wanted and For Rent notices. At a bank of big bay windows overlooking 17th Street there's a counter and barstools for watching the bustling street scene. Local artists' works hang on the walls. Upstairs, there are tables, comfy chairs, a small couch and a TV.

COFFEE: The house specialty is the Toffee Coffee, made with regular drip and caramel-flavored coffees, topped with whipped cream. The hot chocolate and the jumbo cappuccino are served in huge ceramic mugs. There are also 30 flavors of French and Italian sodas made with Stirling and Torani syrups.

FOOD: In the morning, you can get bagels, sticky buns, Rice Krispies treats, muffins, croissants and scones, all from outside purveyors. At lunch there are croissant sandwiches.

CLIENTELE: The Pop Shop attracts a diverse crowd, including lots of gay men from the neighborhood, local business people, and students from nearby Georgetown, George Washington, and American Universities.

BEST COFFEEHOUSES IN THE...

WEST

METRO AREAS

Denver
Los Angeles
Portland
Sacramento
San Diego
San Francisco
Seattle

JITTERS COFFEE N' TEA HOUSE

1523 18th Street

Denver, Colorado 80202 • (303) 298-8490

OPEN 7 A.M. TO MIDNIGHT MONDAY TO FRIDAY;
9 A.M. TO MIDNIGHT SATURDAY; CLOSED SUNDAY.

This Alaskan-themed coffee house in Denver's LoDo (for lower downtown) district has a warm, homey feel, with exposed brick, Native American artwork from the Northwest, and a seating area with two well-stuffed couches. Located in a brick building in the historic district, two blocks from Coors Field, it's got huge industrial windows and incandescent lighting that creates an amber glow. Customers order from the extensive coffee and tea menu at the stacked-log bar. Owner Matt Haggstrom, a videomaker raised in Fairbanks, Alaska, wanted to create an inviting space where local artists and writers could gather and work. Inscribed above the bar is his personal motto: "There is no such thing as failure, only opportunities to learn, break limitations."

COFFEE: Jitters offers four brews—including the Goldminers' Brew and a Kenyan blend—from Java Mountain roasters in Idaho Springs, Colorado. For espresso fiends, there's the quad: four shots of espresso, totaling 32 ounces. There are eight cocoas, five of them imported from Alaska, including Merry Berry, Arctic Amaretto and Tundra Vanilla Spice. The cafe also offers more than 100 teas, listed on a menu board. You can pour your own coffee or let the counter person do it for you.

FOOD: There's a variety of ready-to-go cold foods and pastries, all from outside suppliers. *Westword,* the local alternative newspaper, rated Jitters' pastries the city's best in 1994.

CLIENTELE: In the day, Jitters serves mostly business people and downtown residents. At night, an artsy crowd of musicians, poets, writers and artists takes over.

HENRY ALARMCLOCK, 23, writer, unemployed, Denver:

Alarmclock sits in cafes pondering his generation and writing a novel called "Millenium Sickness." He chose the "Alarmclock" nom de plume four years ago because he wants to offer people a wake-up through his writing, sort of like a strong cup of coffee. Unfortunately, as an artist with no income, he can't afford fancy coffee drinks. He drinks "straight-up coffee, whatever is on hand."

PER DIEM: "Too many." That's 10 cups.

ON WRITING IN A CAFE: "It's like a place where I can participate without participating. I am part of the scene, but I remain separate as a writer. For some reason, being in a cafe gives me my space."

HIS NEW FAVORITE CAFE: Jitters Coffee n' Tea House. This is the place he sneaks away to when he wants to be alone to write. His friends haven't discovered it yet, he says. "This cafe is quite the little gem for me."

Good news for runners: drinking coffee can improve your time. Eighteen runners at Christ Church College in Canterbury, England, tested this hypothesis by running the 1,500 meter race, once after drinking strong coffee and once after drinking decaf. Fourteen of the 18 runners ran faster (an average of four seconds) on the strong stuff.

MUDDY'S JAVA CAFE

2200 Champa Street
Denver, Colorado 80205 • (303) 298-1631
OPEN 4 P.M. TO 4 A.M. DAILY.

Founded in 1974, Muddy's is the granddaddy of Denver coffeehouses. Located in what used to be the "bad" section of downtown, it's a cool hangout for kids too young to go to the bars. There's a lot going on here: In addition to the cafe/espresso bar, there's a used bookstore, a game room with pool table, jukebox and video games, a 60-seat basement theater, even meeting rooms, where life drawing and acting classes and Narcotics Anonymous meetings are held. "It's really a small cultural center," says co-owner Tim Fink. "We ought to get a grant." Funky and full of character, the cafe features rustic wooden beams, wood booths and old tables and chairs, giving the place the air of an old mountain bar. A brick wall is hung with art that changes monthly.

COFFEE: Muddy's serves a great house blend and espresso drinks made with beans from Allegro, a Boulder roaster, in old-fashioned brown mugs. It also has a full soda fountain, featuring malts, milkshakes and ice cream sodas.

FOOD: The food, mostly deli sandwiches, soups and salads, has a great reputation in Denver. You'll also find nachos, burritos, and the espresso board, an assortment of meats and cheeses. Breakfast is served all day and night.

CLIENTELE: Muddy's attracts an alternative crowd, spanning the ages from old beatniks to aging hippies to Generation Xers. Intellectuals come for the cheap books, and teens come to hang out in the game room. Muddy's is also popular with young Europeans staying at the youth hostel down the street.

ANASTASIA'S ASYLUM

1028 Wilshire Boulevard
Santa Monica, California 90407 • (310) 394-7113
OPEN 7 A.M. TO 2 A.M. DAILY.

There's something seductive about Anastasia's. Maybe it's the dim, atmospheric lighting, or the bordello-style furnishings, or perhaps the suggestively named food and drink (Orgasm Cake and Anastasia's Aphrodesiac, for example), but it seems no coincidence that many a romance has started in this popular hangout. The stucco exterior is white, sponge-painted in gold and the cafe's name spelled out in raised gold letters. The bilevel interior is warm and European, with glazed yellow walls and chandeliers. Downstairs, there's an antique walnut bar, red velvet stools and an old couch; upstairs, you'll find a piano, more couches, a church pew, and library desks and lamps for customers who want to read or study. If you get sleepy, you can sack out on one of the sofas and no one will bother you.

COFFEE: The brewed coffee comes from Prebica, the espresso from Illycaffe. Anastasia's offers more than 100 espresso drinks, including the aforementioned Anastasia's Aphrodesiac, made with espresso, steamed milk, vanilla and Irish cream syrups, and whipped cream. For tea lovers, there's the Yogiccino, made with steamed milk and Yogi tea instead of espresso. Anastasia's also serves Jolt Cola and Love Potion, Brainwash and other exotic herbal sodas.

FOOD: Anastasia's caters to vegetarians, serving vegetarian stew, chili, panini and salads. For breakfast, you can order egg-whip steamers (scrambled eggs cooked in the espresso machine), plus decadent muffins and scones from outside suppliers.

CLIENTELE: Anastasia's attracts local musicians, students and Hollywood people, including directors, writers and actors.

MARIAM PARRIS, 22, actress, Santa Monica, California:

Parris was born and raised in London, and her dad was constantly saying, "Let's go to the cafe." She grew up appreciating the smell of coffee and the social ambience of a nice public sitting room, although she never drank coffee until she attended the University of California at Berkeley. She found herself a cafe to call her own as soon as she moved to Santa Monica. (Her dad now runs his own cafe-art gallery in San Jose, California.)

FAVORITE DRINK: Cappuccino.

PER DIEM: Three cups, with an espresso on days she is tired.

FAVORITE CAFE: Anastasia's Asylum. It's great because it is like coffee itself, she says: "Dark and mellow."

PHILOSOPHY: "The most important thing about drinking coffee is everything that goes with it." She loves the friendly atmosphere at Anastasia's so much, she got a job there working as a barista. "It's like my comfort zone. I can relax here."

I'll have a half double decaffeinated half-caf with a twist of lemon.

—Steve Martin, *L.A. Story*

HIGHLAND GROUNDS

742 North Highland Avenue
Hollywood, California 90038 • (213) 466-1507
OPEN 9 A.M. TO 1 A.M. MONDAY TO SATURDAY;
10 A.M. TO 9 P.M. SUNDAY.

This Hollywood coffee joint serves as unofficial commissary for the behind-the-scenes creative types who toil away in numerous nearby film and video post-production facilities. The building it's housed in started out in the '20s as a drive-through rib shack, then went on to become an infamous gay bar named Greg's Blue Dot (also known as The Church). The windowless exterior is distinguished by a beautiful sunset mural painted by one of the employees, who has since gone on to work as a set designer for the Black Crowes. Inside, there is a horseshoe-shaped bar, a huge blackboard for customers to write on, and painful-looking metal furniture designed by another talented staffer. Go up the stairs to a loft that seats 10, or head on out to the sun-drenched patio, complete with firepit and palm trees.

COFFEE: Caffe Latte, a Los Angeles roaster, supplies the coffee and espresso.

FOOD: For breakfast, try the Bulgarian omelette (made with roasted peppers, onion, spinach and feta cheese, topped with chopped walnuts and balsamic vinaigrette) or the Blues Burrito, with scrambled egg, black olives, sausage, cheese, jalapeno peppers and salsa. The lunch/dinner menu includes the black bean burger (a big seller), turkey burger, grilled eggplant sandwich, tacos and burritos.

CLIENTELE: Highland Grounds gets a lot of writers, editors and animators from the nearby studios during the day, rock and roll types at night. Writer/director Quentin Tarentino *(Pulp Fiction, Reservoir Dogs)* is a regular.

ODEON BREADS & PASTRIES

625 A Montana Avenue
Santa Monica, California 90403 • (310) 451-9096
OPEN 6:30 A.M. TO 8:30 A.M. MONDAY TO SATURDAY;
6:30 A.M. TO 6:30 P.M. SUNDAY.

This smart yet unpretentious bakery-cafe is a welcome breath of fresh air on hypertrendy Montana Avenue. Since its 1990 opening Odeon has become a hangout for industry people who come for the freshly baked bread and the refreshing lack of attitude. The interior is warm and sunny, with high ceilings, white marble floor and floor-to-ceiling windows covered with maplewood blinds to filter the afternoon sun. The breads and pastries, all made on the premises, are displayed in cases or on bread racks behind the counter. In the morning, place your order at the counter; at lunch and dinner, however, sit down and a wait person will take care of you. Most days the weather's nice enough to sit on the patio, which is set off by hedges and has green French park chairs and umbrellas. And, miracle of miracles, there's a parking lot next door, so you don't have to circle the block like a buzzard looking for a space.

COFFEE: The excellent house coffee, from Gourmet Coffee Warehouse in Venice, California, is served in china teacups. Odeon also serves basic espresso drinks, plus fresh orange juice and herbal and caffeinated teas.

FOOD: Everything here is made from scratch on the premises. Breakfast includes pastries (croissants, scones and Danish), scrambled egg on a croissant, French toast and design-your-own omelettes. Odeon also makes fat- and sugar-free cinammon rolls, pumpkin-raisin muffins and apricot-date bars. At lunch there are salads, sandwiches and pastas, including penne pasta with grilled vegetables and goat cheese, and spaghetti pomodoro. The desserts range from the prosaic (lemon squares) to the elaborate (chocolate-raspberry mousse cake). And, of course, you can always get wonderful breads and rolls.

CLIENTELE: In addition to the Hollywood screenwriters, actors and execs who come for the low-key atmosphere, Odeon is filled with stroller moms, neighborhood business people and Montana Avenue shopaholics.

PETTERSONS FRISCH ROST

10019 Venice Boulevard
Los Angeles, California 90034 • (310) 839-3359
OPEN 6:30 A.M. TO 11 P.M. SUNDAY TO THURSDAY;
6:30 A.M. TO MIDNIGHT FRIDAY AND SATURDAY

Pettersons is known for its fabulous, free entertainment, particularly Tuesday's open-mike comedy (widely considered the best in town). Located on the border of Culver City, Venice and Los Angeles, this coffeehouse roasts on the premises, and also sells a wide variety of beans and coffee-making accessories. The one-story stucco building is all windows in front, with a green awning that runs around the building and plastic patio furniture on the sidewalk. Inside, there are two separate areas: a small front room with a coffee bar, retail shelves, and counter and stools that run along the window, and a larger space in back with a triangular stage and seating for about 60.

COFFEE: Pettersons, which roasts its own coffee five nights a week and never uses coffee that's more than a week old, serves the house blend (a dark roast) every day, plus a light, decaf and flavored that change daily. It offers a choice of two espressos: the regular, made with a dark roast, and its New Tradition blend, a lighter espresso roast. The house specialty is the Cafe Mocha Blended, a chocolate-coffee milkshake.

FOOD: Pastries, all made by outside bakers, are all you'll find to eat here. There are muffins, croissants, brownies, gingersnaps, chocolate-dipped shortbread, triple chocolate fudge cake, strawberry shortcake, and peanut butter-chocolate chunk cheesecake, to name a few.

CLIENTELE: The crowd here runs the gamut from Sony Studio executives to transvestites and everything in between: local apartment dwellers and students at UCLA (University of California at Los Angeles) and Loyola.

THE BRAZEN BEAN

2075 N.W. Glisan Street
Portland, Oregon 97210 • (503) 294-0636
OPEN 6 P.M. TO MIDNIGHT MONDAY TO THURSDAY;
6 P.M TO 2:30 A.M. FRIDAY AND SATURDAY. CLOSED SUNDAY.

Looking like a set from the old Bette Davis movie "Hush, Hush, Sweet Charlotte," the Brazen Bean is a coffeehouse crossed with a Southern Gothic mansion. Although only open since the end of 1994, this unique spot already has throngs of admirers, who come to lounge in the velvet armchairs, sip the trademark "mocktails" (alcohol-free versions of coffee drinks such as Spanish coffee) and smoke cigars or clove cigarettes in the elegant smoking room. Situated on the main floor of an historic four-story Victorian, the cafe is divided into three rooms: a round, turret-shaped entryway with faux-stone painted walls and a curved wrought-iron bench; a honey-colored parlor with an oversized couch and gilded chairs; and the smoking room, complete with a "smoking menu" of cigars, cigarettes, loose tobacco, pipes and smoking paraphernalia. In politically correct Portland, this is probably the only temple to tobacco; it practically raises smoking to an art form. The Brazen Bean is very much a cafe in the grand European tradition, offering great food, wine, Port and sherry as well as coffee and espresso drinks. This coffeehouse, which doesn't open until 6 p.m., is the kind of place you should visit with a date, not a book.

COFFEE: In addition to coffee and espresso from Sisters Coffee Co., a small roaster in Bend, Oregon, you'll find a big selection of loose-leaf teas. The house specialty is the Chai, a latte-style drink made with Indian tea. If you can't stomach dairy products, ask for a latte made with non-dairy almond milk or vanilla soy. The Brazen Bean recently got a license to sell alcohol; you'll find wines, sherrys, Ports and brandies, as well as martinis, cocktails, Irish coffee and other coffee drinks.

FOOD: Co-owner Bryce Amato, formerly a restaurant chef, makes all the food, including soups, salads, a pesto, cheese and olive sandwich on focaccia, chicken pot pie, and an appetizer plate with three dips—hot artichoke, eggplant, and pesto-sun-dried tomato-feta—with an assortment of breads. The extensive dessert selection includes hot apple crumb pie, chocolate and brandied pear mousse cake, and chocolate fondue for two.

CLIENTELE: The crowd ranges in age from 25 to 45 and includes stockbrokers from the nearby business district, tourists, trendoids, foodies and artsy types.

Portland, Oregon, is home to the world's first 12-step program for coffee addicts. Members of Caffeine Anonymous meet every Friday night to hold hands, discuss their addiction and offer prayers of hope for recovery. As part of the program, members must admit that they are powerless over caffeine and that coffee has made their lives unmanageable.

COMMON GROUNDS COFFEEHOUSE

4321 S.E. Hawthorne Boulevard
Portland, Oregon 97215 • (503) 236-4835
OPEN 6:30 A.M. TO 11 P.M. MONDAY TO FRIDAY;
7 A.M. TO 11 P.M. SATURDAY AND SUNDAY.

Customers vie to sit in the comfy overstuffed chair and two sofas in this smart coffeehouse in the Hawthorne district, a transitional neighborhood of hippies, Generation Xers and working-class types. Housed in a once-dilapidated candy factory, it's definitely a hangout, the relaxed kind of place where people settle in for a couple of hours. The small staff contributes to that feeling; even when the cafe is packed, they don't make you feel as if you ought to hurry up to make room for new arrivals. The tables are small and the chairs a mix from estate sales. On the sidewalk out front, dogs sun themselves while their owners sit on green French bistro chairs and sip espresso at cement-filled birdbaths that serve as tables.

COFFEE: Common Grounds gets its coffee—a dark Palermo roast—from Seattle-based Torrefazione Italia. They do basic cafe drinks—no syrups or flavorings.

FOOD: Owner Michele Wong only serves foods that go well with espresso. She bakes cookies, gingerbread, and mixed berry cobbler using organic fruit (in season). Other baked goods come from local purveyors: bagels from Big Bear Bagels and pastries from the Neighborhood Baking Company. At the counter, you can buy candy, biscotti, and organic apples and bananas.

CLIENTELE: An eclectic mix of business people on their way to work, students from Reed College and Portland State University, moms with kids in tow, the twentysomething crowd, and local police and firefighters. Lots of people arrive on bikes or on foot.

Chocolate Chip Wonders
Common Grounds Coffeehouse, Portland, Oregon

1 stick (8 tablespoons) sweet butter
1/3 cup brown sugar
1/3 cup white sugar
1 cup unsifted flour
1 egg
1/2 teaspoon baking soda
1 cup semisweet chocolate chunks
splash vanilla extract
pinch of sea salt

1. Preheat oven to 325°F.
2. Beat butter and sugars together until creamy. Add egg, vanilla and salt.
3. Sift in flour and baking soda and mix. Add chocolate chunks, then chill dough for at least one hour.
4. Drop dough by spoonfuls onto cookie sheet and bake approximately 8 to 10 minutes until golden.

GIANT STEPS

1208 N.W. Glisan Street
Portland , Oregon 97209 • (503) 226-2547
OPEN 7 A.M. TO 7 P.M. MONDAY TO FRIDAY;
8 A.M. TO 5 P.M. SATURDAY; 8 A.M. TO 3 P.M. SUNDAY.
OPEN UNTIL 9 P.M. ON THE FIRST THURSDAY OF EVERY MONTH.

With smoky '50s jazz playing in the background, Giant Steps is a cool, laid-back espresso bar in the Pearl District, Portland's burgeoning art gallery area. With its minimalist decor, it has little to distract customers from their coffee and their deepest thoughts. Owner Curt Gottfried opened the cafe in 1989 in a space that had once housed an art gallery, and it still looks like one: a long, narrow room with off-white walls, painted wood floor, gallery track lighting, and large windows that fill the room with light. There's seating at a handful of small tables and at the bar, but during the week most people run in and grab their coffee to go. Still, for those who like to linger, the best seat in the house is in the window, which offers great people-watching opportunities. The bar's busiest night is the first Thursday of the month, known in these parts as First Thursday, when the art galleries stay open late to showcase exhibits.

COFFEE: There's coffee from local supplier Longbottom Coffee and Tea, as well as black, green and herbal teas.

FOOD: Because this is defiantly an espresso bar, the food is limited to baked goods—muffins, scones, sweet rolls and fruit tarts—from Panini, a local baker. The only substantial food item available is a spinach ricotta turnover.

CLIENTELE: Owner Gottfied says he knows 99 percent of his customers, most of whom live and work in the neighborhood. There are local business owners and loft dwellers, who tend to be young, creative, and artistic.

RICHARD KURTH, 45, creative director for a snowboard manufacturing company, Portland:

Kurth, awaiting a business contact, recently discovered Giant Steps cafe. "It's hip, artsy," he says, nibbling on his first-ever pine nut cookie and sipping a mocha. However, it was Starbucks, the corporate giant of chain cafes, that first drew him to gourmet coffees several years ago. Starbucks isn't the most eclectic and interesting of cafes, he agrees, but it offers something important to a businessman who appreciates quality control: "You know what you're gonna get."

FAVORITE DRINK: Lattes. A double in the morning, and a single in the afternoon. "I really like this mocha, though," he says of the Giant Steps offering. "Not too sweet, good whipped cream, good coffee flavor."

APPEAL OF CAFES: It's a chance for him and his wife to get away from the kids and indulge themselves. "We like to while away a Sunday morning at a cafe with some scones, read the newspaper and talk adult talk. "What do they discuss? "Oh, once we drink a coffee, we talk about anything."

MEANING OF GOURMET COFFEE: "It's quality of life," he says. "Like drinking red wine. It's special. It's a treat."

Where's my finely ground Kenya blend from Starbucks?

—Frasier Crane, NBC's *Frasier*

TORREFAZIONE ITALIA

838 N.W. 23rd Avenue
Portland, Oregon 97210 • (503) 228-2528
OPEN 6:30 A.M. TO 9 P.M. MONDAY TO THURSDAY;
7 A.M. TO 11 P.M. FRIDAY AND SATURDAY;
8 A.M. TO 9 P.M. SUNDAY. IN THE SUMMER, TORREFAZIONE
CLOSES ONE HOUR LATER EVERY NIGHT.

This cafe in Portland's upscale Northwest neighborhood positively oozes authentic European atmosphere, from the warm, Mediterranean decor to the Italian-accented employees. Torrefazione started out in Seattle in 1986 and branched out to Portland seven years later. Now, it's one of the town's busiest coffeehouses. Located on the corner of Kearny and 23rd in a former movie theater, the cafe has three big windows that open up to let in the breezes. Torrefazione takes a purist approach to its coffee, which is roasted in the Seattle home office: it doesn't serve flavored espresso drinks or syrups. What you get is fabulous coffee, made the Italian way. The espresso is very short (just under an ounce) and creamy; most American coffeehouses pull expressos that are 2 or even 3 ounces. "It's the quality, not the quantity, that counts," says manager Pasquale Madeddu.

COFFEE: Torrefazione has raised espresso pulling to an art. Here, it's thick and creamy, just like in Italy, and the caffe latte is topped with a thick, creamy froth, not the dry foam of many coffeehouses. Another popular drink here is the cioccolata, a hot chocolate so thick it's almost a pudding. In the summer, they serve granita, a slushy cafe latte.

FOOD: Local bakers supply pastries, including croissants, brioche, fruit tarts and cakes.

CLIENTELE: Young professionals from the neighborhood, people who work at nearby Good Samaritan Hospital, young, sophisticated coffee drinkers, and members of the international community.

JAVA CITY

2573 Fair Oaks Boulevard
Sacramento, California 95825 • (916) 488-3303
OPEN 6 A.M. TO 11 P.M. MONDAY TO THURSDAY;
6 A.M. TO MIDNIGHT FRIDAY AND SATURDAY.

This cool, postmodern outpost of coffee chic is one of Sacramento's top spots to socialize. Located just outside the city limits in an upscale shopping mall, Java City has earned a well-deserved reputation for excellent, fresh-roasted coffee. Line up to order at the yellow service counter, then grab a seat; there are plenty of red metal chairs and stainless steel bull's-eye tables, and nobody will mind if you rearrange the furniture to accommodate a large group. The energetic staff can hardly keep up with the morning traffic, but in the late afternoon, when sunlight floods the room through tall windows, this bustling cafe turns into a sleepy study hall. The pace picks up again in the evening, especially Friday and Saturday nights, when the crowd of young revelers spills over into the parking lot.

COFFEE: Java City, which roasts its coffee off site, offers a light, medium and dark roast, plus a decaf, flavored coffee and flavored decaf, all of which change daily. In addition to standard espresso drinks, it serves gelato-based concoctions such as the Fro Mo, made with a shot of espresso and three gelatos (vanilla, chocolate, and cookies and cream), blended like a milkshake and topped with whipped cream and mocha beans.

FOOD: There are brownies, cookies, breakfast pastries, muffins, coffeecake, plus fancy cakes, all made off the premises. You can order premade salads, yogurt, cheeses, and empanadas and burritos (nuke 'em yourself in the microwave). There's a small kitchen that turns out made-to-order sandwiches.

CLIENTELE: The daytime crowd is pretty tame: moms with kids in town, local business folk on their way to work, post-aerobic women in leotards, and students from nearby Sacramento State. At night, the crowd is considerably younger.

DOROTA MADERAK, 18, high school senior, Sacramento, California:

A Polish native who moved here with her family five years ago, Maderak says hanging out evenings at the cafe exposes her to fascinating people, some of them foreigners, each with interesting stories to tell and opinions to share. "Even if you don't agree with them, you can talk with your friends about why they feel that way," she says. "It's so fun. People are so interesting."

FAVORITE DRINK: Tea, but also some French roast. But mainly, she comes to drink up the conversation.

FAVORITE CAFE: Java City, because it is the biggest cafe in town, and has a large outdoor seating area to meet and greet people. It also draws a teenage and twentysomething crowd on weekend nights.

WHAT THE CAFE OFFERS HER: "You learn more about life and about yourself. In high school, people are so set on their goals; they're just striving to get into a good university." But, for her, the cafe is a university. "You meet people who have lived in other countries. It's fun to hear about people's experiences. They are into all kinds of things. People say, 'Oh my gosh, have you seen the Monet exhibition?'"

WHY OTHER TEENS MAY LIKE IT: She has done some peer counseling and notices many teenagers are going through difficult times, feeling alone and stressed. But the cafe allows her to relax, she says. "You know people. They tell you their troubles. It makes you feel not alone. It makes me feel secure."

NEW HELVETIA ROASTERS AND BAKERY

1215 19th Street
Sacramento, California 95814 • (916) 441-1106
OPEN 6:30 A.M. TO 11 P.M. DAILY.

Located seven blocks from California's state capitol, New Helvetia is the matriarch in Sacramento's burgeoning cafe gulch. It's housed in a century-old red-brick firehouse with a sign featuring its mascot: a dalmatian. The hip, halogen-lit cafe, its two-story interior brick walls hung with the work of local artists, is at the same time homey and airy. Just inside the door sits a massive Diedrich roasting machine and an old French luggage cart filled with bags of green beans. The copper-topped tables are large enough to spread open the newspaper, and the comfortable metal chairs are imported from Italy; yet patrons fight to sit in the two oversized rocking chairs, made from redwood wine barrels, in the front window. In the back of the cafe sits a long oak community table, big enough for 10, where business people and local politicians hold court.

COFFEE: The mocha Borgia (chocolate milk with a shot of espresso, topped with lots of whipped cream and orange slices) heads a list of flavored mochas: caramel, cinnamon, hazelnut, vanilla, praline, and raspberry. The cafe also offers 15 hot teas and two iced teas: Orange Pekoe and mango.

FOOD: Next to the counter is a display case crammed with baked goods, all made on the premises: blueberry-lemon scones (served with rich Devonshire cream), blackberry muffins, blackbottom cupcakes, six types of cookies (chocolate chip, oatmeal, snickerdoodles), plus Rice Krispies treats. They also sell cheesecake, cinnamon rolls, apple strudel, banana nut bread, and eclairs. A large chalkboard on the back wall displays the limited but interesting menu. For breakfast, try the firehouse turnover, a triangle of puff pastry filled with fried potatoes, cheddar cheese, eggs and Ortega chilis. Other breakfast winners: eggs steamed in the espresso machine and killer granola. For lunch and dinner, you'll find several sandwiches, served on homemade focaccia, including a vegetarian sandwich (like the hot eggplant and mozzarella version), and the chicken club, made with chicken breast, bacon and Monterey Jack cheese. Soups change daily and might include a hearty vegetable, black bean, or beef stew. There's a couple of hot entrees plus some cold salads.

CLIENTELE: A mix of law students, state government workers, business people, gays and lesbians, tattooed and pierced downtown types, and students.

English coffeehouses were known as "penny universities," because that's how much it cost to get in.

CAFE CREMA

1001 Garnet Avenue
San Diego, California 92109 • (619) 273-3558
OPEN 6 A.M. TO 1 A.M. SUNDAY TO WEDNESDAY;
6 A.M. TO 4 A.M. THURSDAY TO SATURDAY.

This upscale European-style cafe is a pleasantly mellow place by day, but in the evening it undergoes a personality change, becoming one of San Diego's most popular and crowded night spots. Located just three blocks from Pacific Beach, Cafe Crema usually has a line of revelers waiting for entry, with a crowd on the sidewalk and standing room only inside. The large, beautifully appointed space features a curved, wave-like coffee bar of cherrywood and granite, concrete floors, and glass-topped metal tables made by a local artist. If you come early, you may be able to snag one of the comfortable leather armchairs.

COFFEE: An Los Angeles roaster supplies the brewed coffees; Danesi of Italy provides the espresso. Crema serves a regular, flavored and decaf brew, which change throughout the day, plus a wide selection of flavored lattes, made with Monin syrups and served in giant cups. The house specialty is the Creme de la Creme, a blend of four shots of espresso, chocolate, bananas and ice cream, topped with whipped cream and Belgian chocolate shavings. You can also order teas (some served in teapots, others in a cup with an infuser) from the extensive tea menu, or try the Teeccino, a non-caffeinated "herbal espresso" made from nuts and grains that's similar to a caffe latte.

FOOD: Crema's kitchen turns out excellent scones, Danishes, muffins and bagels. The menu, available all day, features soups (the chicken and wild rice is great), salads, pizzas and sandwiches, served on egg or multigrain bread baked in-house. The desserts, from outside suppliers, are fabulous, especially cakes from local baker Extraordinary Desserts, including caramel macadamia nut cheesecake and passion fruit ricotta cake. On Saturdays and Sundays from 9 a.m. to 2 p.m., a chef makes omelettes to order.

CLIENTELE: Crema is crowded with Pacific Beach and La Jolla residents, beachgoers, and students from San Diego State and U.C. at San Diego.

THE LIVING ROOM

1010 Prospect Street
La Jolla, California 92037 • (619) 459-1187
OPEN 7 A.M. TO MIDNIGHT DAILY.

With its comfortable furnishings and ocean view, this coastal coffeehouse is a peaceful, kick-back kind of place. The brick storefront, with its white awning, red neon sign and fenced-off outdoor seating area, is deceivingly small. Inside, you walk past a mirrored wall to order at the coffee bar, then step into The Living Room, which has been outfitted with Victorian loveseats and sofas, Persian rugs atop the tile floor, and antique tables and lamps. The pale yellow, rag-rolled walls are hung with framed maps and antique light fixtures that cast a dim glow. The atmosphere is quiet and pleasant, and the homemade desserts are excellent.

COFFEE: A local roaster supplies the coffees, which include a European house roast, a French roast, a decaf, a flavored and a decaf flavored. The mochas are made with the house hot chocolate, a rich blend of three Swiss chocolates. The large coffee drinks are served in giant latte bowls.

FOOD: In the morning, you can order scones, croissants, Danish, and apple or apricot strudel, plus fresh fruit and granola and a scrambled egg sandwich served on toast, croissant or bagel. At lunch there's quiche, turkey lasagna, chicken pie, beef goulash and cornmeal gnocchi with a red bell pepper sauce. The extensive dessert selection includes mocha mousse cake, chocolate decadence, lemon tart, Black Forest cake and lemon cheesecake.

CLIENTELE: Students from the University of California at San Diego, local business owners and tourists make up the crowd here.

CAFE BORRONE

1010 El Camino
Menlo Park, California 94025 • (415) 327-0830
OPEN 7 A.M. TO 11 P.M. MONDAY TO THURSDAY;
7 A.M. TO MIDNIGHT FRIDAY;
8 A.M. TO MIDNIGHT SATURDAY; 8 A.M. TO 5 P.M. SUNDAY.

This coffeehouse in an affluent suburb of San Francisco has been packed since the day it opened in 1990. A line frequently snakes through the cafe and onto a front courtyard crowded with plastic tables and chairs for those who want to sit outside and enjoy the fine weather. Located about a mile from Stanford University, Borrone's is known for its friendly staff and almost magical atmosphere. It's a clattering, bustling spot inspired by an Italian cafe, with a high, open ceiling, hardwood floors and floor-to-ceiling glass doors that slide open on warm days to create an open-air effect. Owner Roy Borrone, himself an artist, exhibits high-caliber art on the walls; the cafe holds openings every six weeks. The outside courtyard, more like a European plaza with a fountain and seating, is packed, especially on weekends, with people socializing, sunning themselves or reading. (There's a great bookstore, Kepler's, next door.)

COFFEE: The house coffee comes from Graffeo in San Francisco, the espresso from Illycaffe. Borrone's makes the best mocha on the Peninsula; it also serves up a sinful concoction it calls a frosted mocha: espresso, homemade chocolate and coffee ice cream. Wines by the glass are also available.

FOOD: Roy Borrone's wife Rose makes everything from scratch. Breakfast includes simply delicious scrambled eggs, scones (raisin, buttermilk), berry muffins and fresh squeezed juices. For lunch, the cafe serves soups, salads, sandwiches and quiches. A big seller is the chicken salad on toasted raisin bread. Desserts, made on the premises, include vanilla custard and fabulous tiramisu.

CLIENTELE: Borrone's proximity to Silicon Valley and Stanford University makes it a favorite with students, faculty, computer execs, and well-heeled suburbanites.

CAFE FLORE

2298 Market Street
San Francisco, California 94114 • (415) 621-8579
OPEN 7:30 A.M. TO 11:30 SUNDAY TO THURSDAY;
7:30 A.M. TO MIDNIGHT FRIDAY AND SATURDAY.

Located in the heart of the Castro, San Francisco's world-famous gay neighborhood, Cafe Flore attracts a wide cross section of gays and straights. Open since 1977 and modeled on the original Cafe du Flore in Paris, it is a wonderful spot to sit and watch the fabulous parade of characters who cruise down Market Street. Leather men, tourists, bodybuilders, the flamboyantly-dressed transvestite Sisters of Perpetual Indulgence—you can see it all while sipping a cappuccino at an outdoor table at Cafe Flore. There are glass windbreaks around the patio to protect you from the changeable San Francisco weather. Inside, you'll find wood tables with tile inlays and wood cafe chairs. Place your order at the counter; a server will deliver your food.

COFFEE: Cafe Flore gets its coffee from Graffeo and serves one brewed coffee and all the basic espresso drinks. It also has a license to serve beer and wine.

FOOD: In the morning, you'll find frittatas, omelettes, and oatmeal, as well as breakfast pastries. For lunch and dinner, the menu is simple: salads, pastas, burgers and chicken.

CLIENTELE: San Fransicso's gay community claims Cafe Flore as its own. The cafe is expecially popular with European tourists who come for a coffee break after sightseeing on nearby Castro Street.

The ABC-TV show Ellen, *starring comedian Ellen DeGeneris, is set in a bookstore/coffeehouse called Buy the Book.*

CAFFE CENTRO

102 South Park
San Francisco, California 94107 • (415) 882-1500
OPEN 7:30 A.M. TO 6:30 P.M. MONDAY TO SATURDAY; CLOSED SUNDAY.

This cafe is definitely worth a visit, if only for its location. South Park, located south of Market Street, is a charming (and little-known, even among San Francisco residents) European-style park bordered on four sides by restaurants, hotels and small businesses. The area is home to artists, designers, architects and other creative types, giving it the nickname Multimedia Gulch. Caffe Centro, a small but elegant coffeehouse, caters to its artistic neighbors. Housed in the ground floor of a four-story residential hotel on the corner of South Park and Jack London Street, the cafe is architecturally remarkable, the result of a collaboration by local designers and artisans. The outside has a European feel, with green steel tables and chairs just like the ones found in Parisian parks. Inside, the space is divided into two "rooms" by a long center hallway, with butter-colored walls, soft, diffuse lighting, and a wood tile floor that mimics terrazzo flooring. On the right, little paned windows open onto the park, lending the space a romantic air. To the left is the bar, made of upended two-by-fours topped with maplewood and steel. There's also a long standup coffee bar, where someone dining alone can hurriedly down a coffee and panini either standing up or sitting on a stool. For those with a little more time to linger, it's fun to take your coffee across the street and sit on the park grass. On weekdays, there can be 200 or 300 people doing just that.

COFFEE: The coffee, which comes from Mr. Espresso in Oakland, is strong and dark. There's a house blend and classic espresso drinks made the authentic European way. The cafe carries Torani syrups for flavoring, and has a license to serve domestic and imported wines and beers.

FOOD: Chef George Francisco prepares seven or eight versions of gourmet Italian panini daily, including an open-faced sandwich of prosciutto and melted provolone on focaccia, and ripe tomatoes and melted buffalo mozzarella on crunchy Italian bread. There are also soups (try the tomato lobster bisque), salads, and simple, inexpensive, premade panini to go, which sit on the counter. The baked goods are made on the premises and include oat bran muffins, chocolate raspberry scones, cookies and brownies.

CLIENTELE: Cafe Centro attracts a hip, well-dressed, dynamic crowd of people in the visual and electronic arts.

Europe's First Coffee Addict?

When coffee was introduced to Europe, government and religious leaders considered it a sinful libation. But Pope Clement VIII (1536-1605) gave the drink his blessing after trying a cup.

CHANDA WILLIAMS, 39, & BONNIE EVENSON, 35, partners at Palomine Graphic Design, San Francisco, California:

They met only three years ago but quickly became best friends. Both are artistic. Both are from small towns, but had lived in Italy. In fact, they look alike. The design firm they founded in San Francisco's artsy Potrero Hill area is doing well. Oh yes, and both love to linger at a certain cafe over a tall cup of black coffee.

FAVORITE CAFE: Caffe Centro. They like its ethnic and economic diversity.

DAILY RITUAL: Since the pair live in lofts in the same building as their workplace, they like to get out to Caffe Centro for lunch most days of the week. They order gourmet sandwiches, then stretch lunch into the afternoon with tall coffees, sitting at a table by the open window overlooking South Park. "We talk about everything. We run into people we know. We talk about people we see there. Nothing catty," says Williams.

The coffee-loving city of San Francisco celebrates Cafe Arts Month each November.

CAFFE TRIESTE

601 Vallejo Street
San Francisco, California 94133 • (415) 392-6739
OPEN 7 A.M. TO 11:30 P.M. SUNDAY TO THURSDAY; 7 A.M. TO 12:30 A.M. FRIDAY AND SATURDAY.

The Beat Generation put Caffe Trieste on the map back in the '50s, and the spirit of Laurence Ferlinghetti and Allen Ginsberg lives on in this world-famous coffeehouse. The Giotta family, which founded Trieste in 1956 and still runs it, hasn't changed a thing here (and never will); it's still a funky place with Formica-topped tables and coffee bar, a juke box that plays Italian love songs and arias, and hundreds of black-and-white photos of its famous customers on the yellow-orange walls. Located on the corner of Vallejo and Grant streets in the Italian section known as North Beach, Caffe Trieste is as much a San Francisco landmark as Coit Tower or the Transamerica Pyramid. Francis Ford Coppola wrote the screenplay for *The Godfather* here, and countless movies have been shot in and around the shop. The Giottas put on a family concert every Saturday afternoon; it's a standing-room-only affair.

COFFEE: Trieste roasts its own coffee in a 22-kilo roaster, located next door in its retail shop, called Trieste Annex. Trieste serves its coffee strong and makes all its drinks with a double shot of espresso. The latte, served in a clear glass, is beautifully layered, with milk on bottom, coffee on top. The house specialty, Caffe Fantasia, is made with espresso, chocolate, milk, almond syrup, and fresh whipped cream. Trieste also serves beer and wine.

FOOD: The cafe serves assorted pastries, croissants and cookies, made off the premises. Recently, it started serving focaccia sandwiches and pizza, whole or by the slice.

CLIENTELE: The famous, the infamous and the unknown all come to Trieste. North Beach natives stand in line with tourists and yuppies on their way to work in the Financial District.

THE GROVE

2250 Chestnut Street
San Francisco, California 94123 • (415) 474-4843
OPEN 7 A.M. TO 11 P.M. MONDAY TO WEDNESDAY;
7 A.M. TO MIDNIGHT THURSDAY AND FRIDAY;
8 A.M. TO MIDNIGHT SATURDAY; 8 A.M. TO 11 P.M. SUNDAY.

There's something for almost everyone at The Grove: choice coffee, an extensive menu, unusual beers from top microbreweries, excellent people watching, and a cozy place to hang out. It's located in the Marina district, just a few blocks from the bay and home to the city's hip young professionals. The Grove is just one of many restaurants and coffee shops on bustling Chestnut Street, which turns into a veritable street fair on weekends, with fabulous-looking people on foot, bike or in-line skates. Sit at one of the metal tables on the sidewalk and watch the Spandex parade pass by. Inside, the cafe has a Sierra mountain air about it, with antique Mission and Arts and Crafts furnishings, wide wood plank floors, and windows that slide open to create an open-air cafe. There are tables for four, as well as two big tables for eight and a dramatic long oak bench along the wall. The staff won't try to hurry you here; you can sit for hours and read or play one of the games stocked on a nearby shelf.

COFFEE: Illycaffe supplies the espresso beans and Mr. Espresso of Oakland the house coffee, which is served in beautiful New Mexican pottery mugs. Tea comes in a large cast-iron Japanese teapot; there are about 15 bulk teas available. For beer connoisseurs, there are eight microbrewery beers on tap, including Red Nectar Ale and Widmer unfiltered wheat beer from Portland, Oregon. You can also order wines by the glass or bottle.

FOOD: The food (most of it made at an off-premises kitchen) includes toasted bagels, muffins, quiche, granola, frittatas and tortas in the morning, and salads, sandwiches and hot entrees at lunch and dinner. Salads include Thai noodle, papaya-salsa chicken, orzo-feta and a wonderful Caesar. For dessert there're fresh fruit pies, cakes, tortes, brownies, cookies and biscotti.

CLIENTELE: Young, attractive Marina residents come here for food and socializing.

TASSAJARA BREAD BAKERY

1000 Cole Street
San Francisco, California 94117 • (415) 664-8947
OPEN 7 A.M. TO 9 P.M. MONDAY TO THURSDAY;
7 A.M. TO 10 P.M. FRIDAY AND SATURDAY;
8 A.M. TO 9 P.M. SUNDAY.

Tassajara is one of those only-in-San Francisco stories: a bakery cafe, it was founded in 1976 and run by Zen monks, who took time out from their daily baking duties to meditate. That tradition ended in the early '90s, when Tassajara was purchased by Just Desserts, a highly successful San Francisco bakery, but fortunately Tassajara still retains its funky air and reputation for fine breads. Located on the corner of Cole and Parnassus streets in the Upper Haight (also known as Cole Valley), it is a perennial favorite in a neighborhood where cafes and restaurants change hands quickly. There's a scattering of tables and chairs outside, where the smokers and folks with dogs tend to congregate. The cafe features a long glass display case filled with baked goods, and is divided into two seating areas by a low wall and planter box. There's banquette seating along one wall, and the wobbly old tables are crowded close together. Be prepared to share a table with strangers, since this coffeehouse is often packed, especially on weekends and workday mornings.

COFFEE: The coffee comes from Peerless, an Oakland roaster, and includes a single house blend and a full line of espresso drinks. You'll also find natural fruit sodas, Calistoga waters, Odwalla juices and teas from Republic of Tea.

FOOD: The bread is the thing here. Baked fresh daily, it includes loaves (potato, Viennese five-grain, sourdough rye, whole wheat and cottage cheese-dill), four kinds of baguette, and three types of batard, a squat, hearty bread. If you want bread with your coffee, order a demi-baguette or a roll; Tassajara makes all its breads in roll size as well. The baked goods are all made from scratch and include muffins (blueberry, lemon-ginger, orange-pecan), scones, and delicate, buttery croissants. At lunch, there's focaccia, vegetarian soups (try the red potato and leek), and premade sandwiches (choose from cheese-avocado, hummus or tofu). Pastries from Just Desserts include chocolate velvet mousse (three layers of different kinds of chocolate mousse) and chocolate cloud chiffon, a terrine of white, milk, and bittersweet chocolates. For dieters, there's non-fat angel food cake, and organic food lovers will like the Haver cookie, a bar made of rolled oats, apple juice and flour.

CLIENTELE: The entire spectrum of Haight-Asbury residents, from med students to unemployed poets, frequents Tassajara. On weekends, there's stroller gridlock as young families arrive for coffee and pastry.

Cappuccino gets its name from the Cappucine monks of Italy, known for their white-and-coffee-colored robes.

B&O ESPRESSO

204 Belmont Avenue East
Seattle, Washington 98102 • (206) 322-5028
OPEN 7:30 A.M. TO MIDNIGHT SUNDAY TO THURSDAY;
7:30 A.M. TO 1 A.M. FRIDAY AND SATURDAY.

The B&O, which opened in 1976 in the colorful Capitol Hill neighborhood, was one of the original coffeehouses in town, kicking off the coffee craze in Seattle. Now it's literally surrounded by competition, but the B&O remains the undisputed king of coffee here. It started out in a small location behind a tavern, and gradually grew to take over the bar. Located at the corner of Belmont and Olive, it's charmingly atmospheric, with stained glass hanging in the window, an art nouveau mural of a woman carrying a cappuccino, and an enormous floor-to-ceiling antique sideboard in the seating area downstairs. There are two other sitting areas and a pastry room, where you can order more than 30 varieties of fabulous baked goods, which will be delivered to your table by the strongly counterculture staff. Patrons come for the casual, European ambience and the wonderful coffee from Graffeo in San Francisco.

COFFEE: The specialty espresso drinks include the Milky Way (espresso, hot chocolate, homemade caramel and whipped cream) and the white chocolate mocha. B&O also makes great espresso milkshakes using Fratelli ice cream.

FOOD: The kitchen is at work seven days a week producing B&O's signature pastries, including German chocolate cake, sour cream lemon pie, Sacher torte, white chocolate cake, and mocha chew cookies. Scones and muffins are also available.

CLIENTELE: Capitol Hill residents have made the B & O their unofficial clubhouse. You'll find grunge types with chessboards and business people with laptops here. On weekend evenings, the place is packed with people who've just finished eating at one of the area's many restaurants and have come for coffee and dessert.

Mocha Chew Cookies
B&O Espresso, Seattle, Washington

4 ounces unsweetened chocolate
3 cups semisweet chocolate chips
4 ounces unsalted butter
1/2 cup all-purpose flour
1/2 teaspoon baking powder
1/2 teaspoon salt
1 1/2 tablespoons instant espresso powder
4 eggs
1 1/2 cups sugar
2 teaspoons vanilla extract

1. Preheat oven to 350°F degrees.
2. Sift together flour, baking powder, salt and espresso powder.
3. Melt together butter, unsweetened chocolate, and 1 1/2 cups chocolate chips. Set aside remaining chips.
4. Beat eggs, sugar and vanilla until creamy.
5. Fold melted chocolate mixture, sifted dry ingredients, and remaining chocolate chips into egg-sugar mixture. Let mixture rest for 20 minutes to thicken.
6. Drop by tablespoons onto cookie sheets and bake for 15 minutes. Makes about 2 dozen large cookies.

Seattle is home to 10,000 coffee baristas.

BAUHAUS BOOKS + COFFEE

301 East Pine Street
Seattle, Washington 98122 • (206) 625-1600
OPEN 6 A.M. TO 1 A.M. MONDAY TO FRIDAY;
8 A.M. TO 1 A.M. SATURDAY AND SUNDAY.

The view from this Capitol Hill coffeehouse/used bookstore is not the least of its many charms. Sit at the window and you will see the best that Seattle has to offer—glorious mountains and the Space Needle—arrayed before you. Open since late 1993, Bauhaus quickly became a hit with the business set and more bohemian types. The staff is knowledgeable and friendly, the atmosphere comfortable and rustic. Downstairs, there's a big concrete bar and stools, as well as slate tables and old wooden school chairs. If you like a more intimate corner, there's a small room in back with a couple of tables and a booth. On the left wall, bookshelves that reach the ceiling are filled with old books for sale, mostly about art, architecture, design, and the counterculture. You can reach them by climbing a black library ladder. Upstairs, there's balcony seating where you can smoke and enjoy more great views. During the day, the place is bright and sunny, but at night it's dark and moody, with candles flickering in steel wall sconces.

COFFEE: Bauhaus gets its coffee from San Francisco's venerable Caffe Trieste. It also carries bottled soda pops: A&W root beer and cream soda, a German cola, Jolt and the small bottles of Coca Cola and Sprite.

FOOD: They sell coffeehouse pastries made off the premises and, for kitsch value, Ding Dongs.

CLIENTELE: Artists and other bohemians come here to read, write and talk. There's also a lot of teenagers from the local high schools, college students from Seattle Central, and business people from the neighborhood.

CAFE PARADISO

1005 East Pike Street
Seattle, Washington 98122 • (206) 322-6960
OPEN 6 A.M. TO 1 A.M. MONDAY TO THURSDAY;
6 A.M. TO 4 A.M. FRIDAY; 8 A.M. TO 4 A.M. SATURDAY;
8 A.M. TO 1 A.M. SUNDAY.

This busy Capitol Hill coffeehouse, open since 1990, caters to a distinctly young, counterculture crowd. Housed in a two-story renovated warehouse, it's an alcohol-free zone for teens and twentysomethings. The ground floor is dark and beatniky, with dark green faux-finish walls, a couch and a collection of mismatched tables and chairs from Europe, and three chalkboards where customers can express themselves. The espresso bar is staffed by young baristas with various body piercings and non-mainstream hairstyles. But these kids are knowledgeable about coffee; in fact, everyone on the staff must attend an espresso-making clinic every few months. Upstairs, where smoking is allowed, the atmosphere is even more bohemian. There's another espresso bar, complete with stools, and tables and chairs where patrons play cards or chess. Owner Anne Michelson, a self-described aging hippie, presides over the scene like a loving and very non-judgmental mother.

COFFEE: Paradiso serves its coffee, which comes from Olympia roaster Batdorf & Bronson, in huge white ceramic cups. The baristas are expertly trained to pull Italian-style "short" espressos. Customers can help themselves to the house blend from urns on the counter.

FOOD: This cafe serves classic coffeehouse food: homemade, mostly vegetarian fare such as vegetarian chili, hummus and pita, and cream of cauliflower soup. There's also pizza and calzone, chapati (an East Indian tortilla filled with rice and beans), and baked goods made on the premises. Breakfast is served all day long, an idea borrowed from old-style diners.

CLIENTELE: During the day, the clientele runs the gamut. At night, it's packed with young (13 to 30 tops), counterculture patrons who travel from all over Seattle to check out the scene. *Pearl Jam's* Eddie Vedder and *Northern Exposure* actor Rob Morrow have been spotted here.

MIKE FLYNN, 54, publisher of a business newspaper, Seattle, Washington:

A dozen years ago, Flynn tried a latte after dinner in an Italian restaurant. "God, this is good," he thought. He gave up his 12-cup-a-day drip coffee habit, and has never looked back. "Once I had a latte, regular coffee didn't taste good anymore." For awhile, he says, he was one of those Seattle residents who got nervous when flying off on a business trip, wondering how he was going to get his latte fix in the wilds of Chicago or Atlanta. Happily, he says, the rest of America is coming around to gourmet coffee.

Favorite drink: "Let's see. Oh, yes, latte, with no fancy flavorings."

Per diem: Four. First one from an Italian bakery at 6 a.m. while headed to work. Second one from a hotel lobby coffee cart just before his breakfast meeting. Third one from a cart in the afternoon. Fourth one from "any place that's open" on the way home at 7 p.m.

Health angle: Espresso coffees have less acid in them, he says, thus less of a negative health aspect.

He's not a cafe sitter: No time, he says. "Between breakfast and lunch meetings, I gotta get some work done."

Drinking style: "I'm not a sipper. I pause and I drink it. Then I go back to work. I don't know why. It's a pleasurable moment."

On NBC-TV's Frasier, *psychiatrist Frasier Crane hangs out in a Seattle coffeehouse called Cafe Nervosa.*

CAFE SEPTIEME

214 Broadway Avenue East
Seattle, Washington 98102 • (206) 860-8858
OPEN 7 A.M. TO MIDNIGHT MONDAY TO FRIDAY;
9 A.M. TO MIDNIGHT SATURDAY AND SUNDAY.

With its blood-red walls and red vinyl booths, Cafe Septieme has a look you don't find in too many coffeehouses. But that's part of its appeal, along with its outrageous artwork (including some nudes), great food and unpretentious attitude. Owner Kurt Timmermeister opened his first cafe in 1986, then moved to bigger digs in 1990 and 1994 as Septieme's popularity grew. The current cafe, located in what once was a cheesy diner in Seattle's Capitol Hill, is a hybrid: half restaurant, half coffeehouse. There's a diner ambience, but with an elegant twist: white tablecloths and three sets of French doors onto the front sidewalk. After you seat yourself, waiters bring menus and take your order. The food is trendy but good.

COFFEE: The coffee, from Seattle-based Torrefazione Italia, includes the basic espresso drinks: no flavored coffees here.

FOOD: At breakfast there's brioche-raisin French toast, oatmeal with dried sour cherries, and buttermilk biscuits with gravy. For lunch, try the hamburger with tarragon mayonnaise and homemade ketchup, or the roasted eggplant sandwich with olive tapenade on Chiro bread. Dinner is eclectic: pork schnitzel with garlic mashed potatoes and red cabbage, red snapper with saffron rice, and gumbo with andouille sausage and chicken. For dessert, there's Seville cake and a pear and walnut crostada.

CLIENTELE: The crowd spans the ages, occupations and sexual orientations. You'll find doctors having dinner at one table, students drinking coffee at the next.

MONICA CHAE, 24, receptionist/college student, Seattle, Washington:

Chae started drinking lattes and an occasional espresso a few years ago because it kept her going between mornings at work and evenings at college. "It is such a trendy thing to do. All my friends drink coffee. I felt left out. Coffee makes me a nicer person. When I drink coffee, I'm more outgoing. Otherwise I'm pretty shy."

FAVORITE DRINK: Cafe latte.

PER DIEM: Three.

FAVORITE CAFE: Torrefazione Italia.

QUIRK: "I spend more than $100 a month on coffee. Usually, I don't even eat lunch. I just drink coffee."

CAFE STYLE: "I'm usually busy studying. I don't go to socialize. I wear a fake ring so nobody talks to me."

You see, Lainie, this is all we need—a couple of smokes, a cup of coffee and a little bit of conversation. You and me and five bucks.

—Ethan Hawke to Winona Ryder, *Reality Bites*

MACRINA BAKERY AND CAFE

2408 1st Avenue
Seattle, Washington 98121 • (206) 448-4032
OPEN 7 A.M. TO 6 P.M. MONDAY TO SATURDAY;
8 A.M. TO 3 P.M. SUNDAY.

This coffeehouse in Seattle's up-and-coming Belltown neighborhood started life as a bakery, and it still sells the best breads in town. Located in an old waterfront neighborhood that contains both upscale restaurants and homeless shelters, Macrina takes up the ground floor of a modern high-rise apartment building. Outside are hand-crafted signs with the word Bakery and the head of Macrina, a 4th Century Greek mythic figure. Inside, the cafe is modern yet classic, with muted colors and natural materials. The tables have poured concrete tops and hand-forged iron bases; the chairs are made from wood indigenous to the Northwest; and the poured-concrete floor is stained to look like worn leather. There's a concrete bar with stools, where you can watch the chef prepare your lunch. The freshly baked loaves are displayed on old baker's racks, and the daily specials are written on chalkboards on the back wall. In the morning, patrons order and pay at the counter; between 11 a.m. and 3 p.m., however, the cafe shifts gears and turns into a restaurant, with a host to seat you and waiters to take your order and serve. (Between noon and 1:30 p.m. you'll probably have to wait for a table.) Macrina turns back into a self-service coffeehouse in the late afternoons.

COFFEE: Macrina serves organic espresso and teas from Kalani, a small local roaster. If you want brewed coffee, order the Americano: two shots of espresso with water added. In early 1995 the cafe got a license to sell wine and beer.

FOOD: The breads are the main attraction: There's a dense, chewy sourdough, a classic crusty Italian loaf, and a wonderful potato bread. For breakfast you can also get homemade fat-free granola, citrus and oat scones, a classic sour cream coffee cake made with low-fat yogurt, and the ficelle, a 10-inch baguette served with butter and jam. The lunch menu, which changes daily, features soup, organic mixed greens salad, and a hot entree: perhaps risotto with butternut squash, or a roasted half chicken served with garlic mashed potatoes. In the afternoon, try the mezze, a selection of Mediterranean hors d'oeuvres. Desserts are elaborate and European; try the crepes, the creme caramel or the seasonal fruit tart.

CLIENTELE: The business crowd and shoppers from the nearby retail district eat lunch here, while upscale residents drop by for coffee and bread and hikers and bikers come to load up on provisions. Tourists haven't discovered this gem—yet.

Say, "Ahhhhh."

Seattle boasts the country's first cafe/dentist office. At Espresso Dental, you can order a cappuccino or latte before your teeth-cleaning.

Breakfast Bread Pudding
Macrina Bakery and Cafe, Seattle, Washington

1 1/2 cups milk
1/2 cup heavy cream
2 eggs, plus 2 egg yolks
1 teaspoon vanilla extract
3/4 cup honey
pinch of cinnamon
1/2 cup butter, melted
good quality white bread, cut into 1/2 inch cubes to make 6 1/2 cups cubes
6 ripe apricots, chopped (you can substitute other fruit in season)
1/2 cup thick cut oats
1/4 cup chopped walnuts
cinnamon-sugar mixture (recipe below)
fresh fruit sauce (recipe below)

1. Preheat oven to 325°F. Butter a 2-quart baking dish.
2. Prepare custard in large bowl by whisking together milk, cream, eggs, yolks, vanilla and 1/2 cup honey.
3. Toss cubed bread with melted butter and cinnamon-sugar mixture.
4. Toss the chopped apricots with remaining 1/4 cup honey and add to the bread mixture.
5. Place bread mixture in buttered baking dish and pour custard mixture over it. Top with oats and chopped walnuts.
6. Bake for 1 hour. Serve warm with fruit sauce.

To make cinnamon-sugar mixture:

Combine 2 tablespoons brown sugar, 2 tablespoons granulated sugar, and 1 teaspoon cinnamon.

Fresh Fruit Sauce:

Combine 4 cups fresh fruit (berries, apricots or peaches), 1/2 cup sugar, 1 teaspoon lemon juice, and 1 tablespoon cinnamon in a saucepan and bring to a simmer. Cook for 5 minutes. Taste. If not sweet enough, add sugar. Continue cooking until fruit is tender.

BEST COFFEEHOUSES IN THE...

MIDWEST

METRO REGIONS

Chicago
Cincinnati
Columbus
Detroit
Indianapolis
Milwaukee
Minneapolis–St. Paul

GREEN MOUNTAIN COFFEE ROASTERS

131 West Jefferson
Naperville, Illinois 60540 • (708) 355-6444
OPEN 6 A.M. TO 10 P.M. MONDAY TO THURSDAY; 6 A.M. TO 11 P.M. FRIDAY AND SATURDAY; 7 A.M. TO 10 P.M. SUNDAY.

This cafe in an upscale suburb of Chicago is part of a New England chain of roaster-coffeehouses. Located in a charming turn-of-the-century brick building that used to house the police and fire stations, Green Mountain caters to people who shop and work in this quaint and heavily trafficked downtown area. Outside, there are green awnings and cafe tables with large green umbrellas. Inside, there are twin focal points: a slate water fountain on one side of the cafe, a Sasa-Samiac coffee roaster on the other. The ambience is woodsy and natural, with pine tables, a hardwood floor, and walls painted hunter green. Coffee is stored in burlap bags on the floor and in a bank of glass bins filled with 28 varieties of coffee beans; you can lift up the lids to smell the heady aroma before purchasing. The 12-foot-long coffee counter jags along the wall; there, you'll find display cases of baked goods. Bright track lighting and the strains of classical music on the sound system add to the relaxing atmosphere.

COFFEE: A solicitous barista will inquire about your coffee preferences before offering one of seven brewed coffees available daily. Coffee is served in clear glass mugs, and refills are free. In addition to the standard espresso drinks, there's a house specialty called the Mocha Almond Chiller: espresso, almond flavoring, ice and chocolate milk, blended to a slushy consistency. Green Mountain roasts its coffees on the premises.

FOOD: At the counter you can order freshly baked croissants, cookies and muffins. The menu is basic coffeehouse fare: soups, salads and croissant sandwiches. Desserts (which are made off the premises) include several types of cheesecake and tiramisu.

CLIENTELE: This is an upscale yuppie hangout full of business types on their way to work and mothers with babies in strollers. Students from nearby North Central College come here to study.

KOPI, A TRAVELER'S CAFE

5317 North Clark Street
Chicago, Illinois 60640 • (312) 989-5674
OPEN 8 A.M. TO 11 P.M. MONDAY TO THURSDAY;
8 A.M. TO MIDNIGHT FRIDAY; 9 A.M. TO MIDNIGHT SATURDAY;
10 A.M. TO 11 P.M. SUNDAY.

This travel-themed cafe in Chicago's trendy Andersonville neighborhood is designed to appeal to wanderlusting souls. It's actually a travel bookstore and Third World boutique (selling clothing, jewelry and art) as well as a coffeehouse, where patrons can spread out maps and plan exotic trips to the accompaniment of World Beat music on the sound system. Remove your shoes before ascending to a raised platform to lounge on floor pillows at low tables; Kopi provides house slippers should you wish to walk around the store. There's also conventional seating at tables and chairs near the coffee counter. Table service is provided by friendly, helpful staffers.

Coffee: A local roaster supplies Kopi, which serves a house blend, a flavor of the day, and a decaf, usually a dark roast. There's an extensive menu of espresso-based drinks and teas, as well as Mexican hot chocolate and Viennese coffee.

Food: The baked goods, from an outside supplier, include bagels, scones, muffins and desserts such as carrot cake and chocolate espresso cake. The largely vegetarian menu features soups (gazpacho, mushroom-barley), salads, sandwiches and focaccia.

Clientele: Kopi attracts an adventurous crowd of travelers of both the real and armchair varieties. Some come to plot upcoming trips (there's a filing cabinet full of travel resources), others just to fantasize. There's also a sizeable contingent of local artists, residents and students from nearby Loyola, DePaul, and the University of Chicago.

SCENES COFFEE HOUSE AND DRAMATIST BOOKSTORE

3168 North Clark Street
Chicago, Illinois 60657 • (312) 525-1007
OPEN 10 A.M. TO 11:30 P.M. MONDAY TO THURSDAY;
10:30 A.M. TO 2:30 A.M. FRIDAY AND SATURDAY;
10:30 A.M. TO 11:30 P.M. SUNDAY.

Four blocks from Wrigley Field, this tiny cafe and bookstore is both a neighborhood hangout and a place for actors and other theater types to congregate. The walls are covered with books about theater and film, and the cafe bears lots of theatrical touches: stage lights, a callboard for auditions and performing arts notices, and a small stage for poetry readings and performances. The atmosphere is warm and comfortable, with the feel of a '60s coffeehouse. There are only 10 tables, and the place gets crowded after the theater. Because seating is limited, be ready to share your table during rush hour.

COFFEE: Try the espresso milkshake and the Jamie Special (named after co-owner Jamie Asch): an iced double espresso, mixed with half and half and coffee-flavored Torani syrup, topped with steamed milk.

FOOD: This is one of the few places in the area that offers a civilized meal late at night. The menu is pricey by cafe standards. In addition to the standard muffins and scones (not baked on the premises), it offers 13 sandwiches, including a great vegetarian burger on an onion dill roll, served with celery root remoulade on the side.

CLIENTELE: Young artists, writers, neighborhood yuppies, retirees from nearby Lakeshore Drive, and gays. There's also a strong contingent of high school kids and college students from DePaul, Columbia College and Art Institute of Chicago.

LYNN ALLEN, thirtysomething male, TV producer, Chicago, Illinois:

Allen, who is working on a TV show about cafes around the world, loves to sit at the big picture window up front at Scenes Coffee House, watching the world outside and inside. "Scenes is a scene. I'm people watching, I guess it's research. My philosophy is we're all students in life." But, at least on one occasion, he did more than watch. He picked a woman up, or she picked him up. He's not sure.

FAVORITE DRINK: Cappuccino, frothy.

PER DIEM: "I've had four so far. That's typical."

HIS TV RESEARCH SHOWS: "In Paris, the cafe chairs often are all lined up facing the street, like sitting at a movie theater. Even if you sit with someone, you don't look at each other, you regard the street. In America, you sit face to face."

CAFES AS PICKUP PLACES: "Sure, there is definitely the opportunity." Not so long ago, he asked to share a table on a crowded day with a young woman. She asked him about the book he was reading, and the conversation led to a dating relationship that lasted some months, he says. "A cafe is not a meat market. There are unspoken ground rules," he says. "In cafes, you are open to talking, but you shouldn't bother anyone."

America has more than 5,000 cafes and coffeehouses. That number is expected to double by the year 2000.

UNICORN CAFE

1723 Sherman Avenue
Evanston, Illinois 60201 • (708) 332-2312
OPEN 7 A.M. TO 11 P.M. MONDAY TO THURSDAY;
7 A.M. TO MIDNIGHT FRIDAY; 7:30 A.M. TO MIDNIGHT SATURDAY;
7:30 A.M. TO 11 P.M. SUNDAY.

College students, professors and business people crowd this cafe in an old converted warehouse in downtown Evanston, just one block from Northwestern University. Visiting there is like hanging out in a friend's kitchen: kicked back and unpretentious. The decor leans towards light and natural, with hardwood floors, marble-topped tables and soothing beige walls hung with art from local artists. Local celebs, including actor-siblings Joan and John Cusak and Illinois Senator Paul Simon, are sometimes spotted there.

COFFEE: They roast their own coffee at their retail and bulk coffee store about a mile away. Try the Unicorn, a shot of cold espresso mixed with a scoop of vanilla ice cream, cold milk and whipped cream. But you won't find flavored coffees here.

FOOD: Muffins, bagels, scones, cheesecakes, Bundt cakes and cookies are made off the premises. There's also a soup of the day, vegetarian panini, and turkey and cheddar on a croissant.

CLIENTELE: During the day, local businesspeople and professors from Northwestern: at night a rowdier crowd of students comes to hang out, study and socialize.

The Turks used to call cafes "schools for the wise."

AWAKENINGS COFFEE & TEA CO.

2734 Erie Avenue
Cincinnati, Ohio 45208 • (513) 321-2525
OPEN 7 A.M. TO 10 P.M. MONDAY TO WEDNESDAY;
7 A.M. TO MIDNIGHT THURSDAY AND FRIDAY;
8 A.M. TO MIDNIGHT SATURDAY AND SUNDAY.

This bright, spotless cafe was a hit when it opened in late 1992, providing a casual, comforting refuge for well-heeled locals taking a break from business or shopping. Located in Cincinnati's upscale Hyde Park Square, it's got clean-cut, Starbucks-style ambience: lots of white oak, hardwood floors and chalkboards listing the coffees available that day. The white walls are hung with burlap coffee bags and the work of a local artist. Customers place their orders at the counter and seat themselves at small tables. At the back of the shop there's a retail area, with coffee, teas, gourmet food items and coffee-making paraphernalia for sale. One of the few non-smoking coffeehouses in Cincinnati, Awakenings caters to an upscale crowd who come for the cozy atmosphere, polite service and good pastries.

COFFEE: Awakenings gets its coffee from several West Coast roasters. The house blend is a combination of Guatemalan, Colombian and French roasts; a flavored brew and a coffee of the day are also available. The cafe offers basic espresso drinks, served in clear mugs.

FOOD: The desserts, made off the premises by local bakers, include chocolate decadence, white chocolate cheesecake and brownies. For breakfast, there are scones, croissants and other French pastries. The cafe does not serve lunch or dinner.

CLIENTELE: The regulars include upscale Hyde Park residents, business folk and shoppers. In the evening, dim lighting and romantic atmosphere attract couples on dates.

KALDI'S COFFEEHOUSE AND BOOKSTORE

1204 Main Street
Cincinnati, Ohio 45210 • (513) 241-3070
OPEN 8 A.M. TO 1 A.M. MONDAY TO THURSDAY;
7 A.M. TO 2:30 A.M. FRIDAY; 10 A.M. TO 2:30 A.M. SATURDAY;
10 A.M. TO MIDNIGHT SUNDAY.

With its restored antique tin ceiling, weathered hardwood floors and old diner booths, Kaldi's looks and feels as if it's been around forever (though it opened in 1992). The bookshop/cafe is located in the poetically named Over the Rhine section of Cincinnati, an old German settlement that's become a magnet for art galleries and trendy restaurants. Here, what passes for counterculture in this Midwest city gathers to smoke, drink espresso and thumb through the used books that line the walls. Patrons also come for the nightly entertainment and the booze—Kaldi's has a liquor license and stocks a full bar. For the best seat in the house, wander back though the narrow store to the cozy reading room.

COFFEE: Kaldi's gets its coffee from two local roasters, Seven Hills and Queen City. It offers a house blend, two flavored blends, a Colombian decaf and a coffee of the day. Thanks to its liquor license, Kaldi's also serves alcoholic coffees, such as Irish coffee, Angel Cloud (Sambuca, coffee and whipped cream) and Millionaire's coffee (made with four liqueurs).

FOOD: The menu is simple and leans towards the vegetarian: quesadillas, red beans and rice, eggplant lasagna, and Kaldi's unburger (a meatless burger). For breakfast, you'll find basic fare such as French toast, scrambled eggs, and an assortment of muffins, scones, croissants and bagels. Most of the desserts are made off the premises, but the kitchen does turn out a good bread pudding and fruit cobbler.

CLIENTELE: Students from nearby University of Cincinnati and Xavier University come to study during the day, party at night. There's also a diverse crowd of business types and artists from the neighborhood.

CUP O' JOE

627 South Third Street
Columbus, Ohio 43206 • (614) 221-1563
OPEN 7 A.M. TO 11 P.M. MONDAY TO THURSDAY;
7 A.M. TO 1 A.M. FRIDAY; 8 A.M. TO 1 A.M. SATURDAY;
8 A.M. TO 11 P.M. SUNDAY.

This coffee-cum-dessert house in Columbus' charming historical district combines post-modern industrialism with the warmth of wood and brick. Located in a glass-fronted, century-old storefront, Cup o' Joe is sandwiched between an art gallery and a highly regarded bookstore. Outside there's seating for about 25 on the wide, European-style sidewalk, where pedestrians amble on their way to area restaurants, antique shops and pubs. Inside, you'll find wood floors, a sky-blue ceiling and a Picasso-esque mural. Coffee sold by the pound is stored in bins that fill up a wall. Order from the large menu board at the perforated-metal coffee bar, then choose a seat at a wood table or the counter. But the best spot in the house is in a small area up front with a velour-covered couch and two easy chairs.

COFFEE: The extensive coffee menu includes six brewed coffees and about 20 espresso drinks, such as the Milky Way (espresso, chocolate, caramel and steamed milk, topped with whipped cream and shaved Belgian chocolate) and the Razzmatazz (espresso, chocolate, raspberry flavoring, steamed milk, whipped cream and chocolate). In the summer, try the Joe Cool (house blend coffee with vanilla syrup and half and half over ice) or the Iced Mocha Joe (espresso with chocolate milk over ice, topped with whipped cream). Non-coffee specialties include Hot Apple Pie, a spiced hot apple cider, and the Creamsicle, made with orange juice, vanilla syrup and half-and-half.

FOOD: The emphasis here is on desserts, some made on the premises, others brought in from bakers in Chicago, California and New York. There's the devilishly rich chocolate truffle cheesecake from New York's Carnegie Deli, as well as raspberry blackout cake and deep-dish caramel apple pie. The breakfast pastries, made in house, include muffins (blueberry cream is a specialty), croissants, pecan and cinnamon rolls, scones, cookies and three kinds of brownies. For lunch, there's soups, sandwiches and quiches.

CLIENTELE: The crowd ranges from young trendies to conservative older folks, plus tourists and students from nearby Capital Law School.

Coffee should be black as hell, strong as death, and sweet as love.

—Turkish proverb

STAUF'S COFFEE ROASTERS

1277 Grandview Avenue
Columbus, Ohio 43212 • (614) 486-4861
OPEN 8 A.M. TO 10 P.M. MONDAY TO THURSDAY;
8 A.M. TO 11 P.M. FRIDAY; 9 A.M. TO 11 P.M. SATURDAY;
10 A.M. TO 4 P.M. SUNDAY.

Stauf's had only four seats when it opened its doors as a coffee roaster/cafe in 1987. But as its reputation grew, so did the coffeehouse, which now has seating for almost 100. Columbus' first coffeehouse, it practically owns the wholesale market here, providing coffee for dozens of restaurants. Its four in-house roasters are kept busy non-stop, perfuming the coffeehouse with the great smell of roasting beans. Located in a historic building in the center of town, Stauf's has a large glass storefront, green awnings, and bike racks for customers. Inside, the building is divided into a retail space, with barrels filled with 112 types of coffee and shelves of brewers, mugs and tea makers. Walk through a wide portal and you're in the coffeehouse proper, a large, inviting space with wood floors, high ceilings and brick walls covered with coffee maps and burlap coffee bags. Wend your way past the dark wood tables and chairs to the coffee bar, with its pastry display cases and two double-headed espresso machines. Knowledgeable baristas will prepare your coffee, which you can drink inside or out.

COFFEE: The coffee, roasted on site, includes four brews that change daily, plus basic espresso drinks. In the summer, try the coffee cooler, made with strong coffee, milk, sugar and vanilla. Stauf's also stocks 60 varieties of tea.

FOOD: Stauf's makes almost everything on premises, including scones, bagels, croissants, brioche, and French-style pastries. The espresso mocha cheesecake is superb. For lunch, there are premade sandwiches available.

CLIENTELE: The cafe attracts coffee aficionados from all over, as well as business people with laptops, local college kids, chess players and the stroller set.

BRAZIL COFFEEHOUSE

305 South Main Street
Royal Oak, Michigan 48067 • (810) 399-7200
OPEN 9 A.M. TO MIDNIGHT SUNDAY TO THURSDAY;
9 A.M. TO 3 A.M. FRIDAY AND SATURDAY;
9 A.M. TO MIDNIGHT SUNDAY.

You'll have to come early if you want a seat on one of the silk-covered sofas in this sophisticated, stylish cafe in an upscale suburb of Detroit; there's a line to get in every night. The place is run along the lines of a restaurant, with a hostess to seat you and waiters to take your order. Located in a narrow, windowed storefront, the cafe has bar seating and wood tables and chairs in addition to the eight plush sofas. The interior is modern and spare, with a long, concrete-topped counter, 40-foot Brazilian-inspired mural, baby grand piano and long panels of burlap hanging from the ceiling. If you're just looking for a quick cappuccino, go to the retail area in the front of the shop, where a well-trained barista prepares orders to go. Otherwise, sit back and let the staff pamper you.

COFFEE: Brazil carries 20 varietals from Gourmet Coffee, a local roaster. It serves the Brazil roast house blend (a combination of Sumatra, Java and Kenya AA beans), plus a blend that changes daily. The espresso drinks are layered and served in clear glasses. House specialties include the Brazilian Mudslide and the Brazilian Supreme.

FOOD: Almost everything is made off the premises. The breakfast pastries include scones (try the white chocolate-raspberry or the non-fat cranberry), muffins, bagels and biscotti. For lunch there are soups, quiches and sandwiches, such as the Michigan turkey salad, made with chunks of turkey breast, raisins, apple and mayonnaise, served on a croissant. Brazil also serves empanadas, chicken strudel, hummus, and South American black bean dip with blue corn chips. There's an extensive dessert selection that includes chocolate-banana-Bailey's torte and Key lime pie.

CLIENTELE: This sophisticated coffeehouse attracts a thirtysomething clientele of gays and straights, including shoppers, business folk and diners from nearby restaurants.

GOTHAM CITY CAFE

22848 Woodward Avenue
Ferndale, Michigan 48220 • (810) 398-7430
SUMMER: OPEN 5 P.M. TO 2 A.M. MONDAY TO THURSDAY;
2 P.M. FRIDAY TO 2 A.M. SUNDAY.
WINTER: OPEN 5 P.M. TO 2 A.M. MONDAY TO THURSDAY;
5 P.M. TO 6 A.M. FRIDAY; NOON TO 6 A.M. SATURDAY;
NOON TO 2 A.M. SUNDAY.

With its hole-in-the-wall exterior and dark, funky interior, this cafe won't win any design awards. But what it lacks in aesthetics it more than makes up for in personality. Located in an artsy northern suburb of Detroit, Gotham City is the kind of place where the owner thoughtfully repaints the bathrooms every few weeks to give the graffiti artists a fresh canvas. It's reminiscent of a '60s-vintage Greenwich Village coffeehouse, with its mix-and-match tables and chairs, dim lighting, shelves of old books and a stage where local poets and musicians perform every night but Mondays. There's a couple of couches and cushy chairs where the mostly young clientele hang out, smoke cigarettes and consume a lot of Jolt Cola in a friendly, accepting atmosphere.

COFFEE: The coffee comes from local roaster Paramount Coffee. House specialties include the Red-Eye, made with three shots of espresso, flavored syrup of your choice, milk and whipped cream, and the Caffeine Killer, a heart-stopping combination of hot coffee, cold Jolt Cola and ginseng extract that was concocted by a regular customer named Big Joe. Gotham City also carries teas, ginseng-based beverages, and apple and ginger brew.

FOOD: Basic coffeehouse fare is available: soups, sandwiches, cookies and muffins, all prepared off the premises.

CLIENTELE: Gotham City attracts a lot of young poets and musicians and aging hippies.

GRATZI COFFEE HOUSE & CLASSIC CAFFE

222 South State Street
Ann Arbor, Michigan 48104 • (313) 741-4445
OPEN 7 A.M. TO MIDNIGHT MONDAY TO SATURDAY;
8 A.M. TO MIDNIGHT SUNDAY.

Ann Arbor, home to the University of Michigan, boasts more coffeehouses per square mile than any other spot in Detroit. But Gratzi stands out in the crowd. Located on the ground floor of an office building on the edge of campus, this cafe serves the best coffee in town. (It's roasted at a nearby facility.) It looks like a cozy student union, with floor-to-ceiling windows and wood floors, a U-shaped coffee bar, plus plenty of tables and chairs packed closely together. When the weather's nice, they put chairs and tables out on the sidewalk along the side of the building. Gratzi is one of the few coffeehouses in town that allows smoking.

COFFEE: Gratzi roasts its own coffee at an off-site facility. The house coffee and the espresso are made from a flavorful blend of Colombian Supremo, Mexican, Brazilian and Sumatran beans that's not too strong or bitter. Gratzi also serves three flavored coffees that change daily. House specialties include the Cafe Mocha, prepared with a homemade chocolate sauce, and the Lampone, a raspberry-flavored cappuccino. In the summer, try the slushy Cappuccino Frappe.

FOOD: You'll find muffins, croissants, pecan rolls, bagels, cookies and brownies. The apple streusel muffin and the white chocolate raspberry scone are terrific. For lunch, you can order quiche, soup, or submarine sandwiches. Desserts include fruit flan, Black Forest torte and cheesecakes. Everything is made off the premises.

CLIENTELE: Students, students and more students.

PLANET ANT COFFEEHOUSE

2357 Caniff
Hamtramck, Michigan 48212 • (313) 365-4948
OPEN 7 A.M. TO 1 A.M. MONDAY TO THURSDAY;
7 A.M. TO 3 A.M. FRIDAY; 7 P.M. TO 3 A.M. SATURDAY;
7 P.M. TO 1 A.M. SUNDAY.

You can't miss Planet Ant, with its bright green brick exterior and big glass storefront. Its devoted regulars aren't fazed by the strange hours it keeps (open in the morning and evening, closed in the middle of the day), but first-timers can always check to see if the green neon OPEN sign is illuminated. Located in Hamtramck, a tiny city within Detroit that's home to both Eastern European transplants and young artists and students, Planet Ant has a retro feel, a strong counterculture edge and a sense of humor: The interior was originally supposed to include a wall-length ant farm called Planet Ant. The ant farm never came to be, but the name stuck. Instead, the design features a high tin ceiling painted bright green, old chrome tables and chairs, and vinyl-upholstered couches and kidney-shaped coffeetables from the '50s. The lighting is dark and atmospheric, punctuated by Christmas lights that twinkle all year long. The patio out back has umbrella-topped cement tables and adorned chairs with gothic-looking ant-eating demons, made by a local artist.

Coffee: Order espresso or coffee (house or the flavor of the day) at the glass and wood bar. Planet Ant flavors its espresso drinks with Torani syrups, and in the summer does a big business in Thai iced coffee and French and Italian sodas. The house special is the Cockroach, a triple espresso plus a double coffee that's especially popular with students during finals week.

Food: Everything's homemade. In the morning there are bagels and muffins; later you'll find spinach pie, hummus, gourmet mini-pizzas, and desserts (chocolate chip brownies, cheesecake).

Clientele: Planet Ant gets lots of students from Wayne State University and the University of Detroit, as well as local artists and musicians. In the morning, business people come in for their coffee to go.

THE ABBEY COFFEEHOUSE

771 Massachusetts Avenue
Indianapolis, Indiana 46204 • (317) 269-8426
OPEN 8 A.M. TO 1 A.M. MONDAY TO THURSDAY;
10 A.M. TO 2 A.M. FRIDAY AND SATURDAY;
10 A.M. TO 1 A.M. SUNDAY.

With a winking reference to organized religion, The Abbey has booths made out of church pews and New Agey Gregorian chants playing in the background. Housed in a handsome brick and glass building in the historic Chatam's Arch district in downtown Indianapolis, this coffeehouse has the tranquil air of someone's living room. The furnishings include an antique sofa, old oak tables, and 25 velvet wing-back chairs along the window, where you can do some serious people-watching. But regulars fight over the very private, corner window seat.

COFFEE: Panache, a Portland, Oregon, roaster, provides the coffee. Choose from a medium and dark roast, decaf, flavored brew, and a decaf flavored coffee. You'll also find some excellent organic teas.

FOOD: The Abbey makes most of its pastries, including muffins, scones and Danish. There's a bacon and egg strudel for breakfast, and sandwiches and salads at lunch. Desserts include chocolate raspberry cheesecake, creme brulee, key lime pie, and ten-layer chocolate torte.

CLIENTELE: The crowd is a mixed bag of young and old, students, business people and families.

Look here, Steward, if this is coffee, I want tea; but if this is tea, then I wish for coffee.

—English Punch magazine, 1902

THE VILLAGE IDIOT

6360 Guilford Avenue
Indianapolis, Indiana 46220 • (317) 257-5556
OPEN 7 A.M. TO 9 P.M. MONDAY TO THURSDAY;
7 A.M. TO MIDNIGHT FRIDAY;
8 A.M. TO MIDNIGHT SATURDAY; 9 A.M. TO 9 P.M. SUNDAY.

This hip little cafe-eatery in the artsy Broad Ripple section of Indianapolis pulls off a nifty combination: It serves restaurant-caliber food in a relaxed coffeehouse atmosphere. The Village Idiot is located on the ground floor of a green three-story Victorian that has a sweeping wraparound porch with outdoor seating during the warm months. Inside, there are three separate rooms, each with the original wood trim and floors, that are furnished with antique chairs and tables, old-fashioned ceiling fans, and lots of greenery. The plain white walls serve as backdrops for rotating art exhibits. If you want to grab a coffee to go, there's a service counter in the back; otherwise, sit down and let a server take your order. The baked goods are scrumptious, and the espresso is the strongest in town.

COFFEE: The Village Idiot, which gets its coffee from several suppliers, offers six brews daily. House specialties include the Nutty Idiot, made with espresso, chocolate, almond and coconut flavorings and steamed milk, topped with whipped cream, and the Green Idiot, flavored with creme de menthe and creme de cacao.

FOOD: The on-site bakery pulls out all the stops with a large selection of homemade desserts, pastries and biscotti. Try the brownies (cream cheese, cherry, or espresso), and the scones, both sweet (apple-cinnamon) and savory (cheddar and bacon). There's also a full breakfast menu, available all day long, including French toast, pancakes, homemade granola, and eggs steamed in the espresso machine. For lunch, the menu tends towards vegetarian fare: black bean soup, hummus, gourmet grilled cheese, and veggie burgers. The dinner menu features pasta and rice dishes. To finish it all off, there are wonderful American desserts: carrot cake, cheesecake, pies and cookies.

Clientele: This cafe attracts mostly people who live and work in Broad Ripple, an artistic community that's been compared to Greenwich Village. Local bookstore and boutique owners, shoppers, massage therapists, artists, and staffers from the nearby alternative newspaper come for the good food and the relaxed atmosphere.

Trivia Quiz: How did Starbucks Coffee Company get its name?

Answer: From the first mate in Herman Melville's Moby Dick, who knew the difference between a coffee pot and an oil can.

FUEL CAFE

818 East Center Street
Milwaukee, Wisconsin 53212 • (414) 374-3835
OPEN 9 A.M. TO MIDNIGHT DAILY.

This is the spot for Milwaukee's alternative and subculture crowds. Located on a desolate street in an ethnically mixed, bohemian part of town called River West, Fuel Cafe attracts a young, artsy clientele who aren't put off by the neighborhood's bad reputation. The 70-year-old brick building still has the original green and white checked floor and tin ceiling, and one wall has been painted with an enormous graffiti-style mural. Fuel Cafe's owners furnished the place on a shoestring with old chrome chairs and Formica-topped tables found on curbsides and at Salvation Army stores, making the place resemble a really cool thrift store. The place is filled with the haze of cigarette smoke and loud, punk music. For your reading pleasure, there's a rack of alternative magazines and comic books.

COFFEE: The excellent coffee, from local Alterra Coffee Roasters, is served in mismatched diner mugs. Help yourself to 25-cent refills from air-pots near the counter. The espresso drinks menu includes the Kervorkian Krush, a 16-ounce latte glass with four shots of espresso, one shot of hot chocolate, and house coffee.

FOOD: Fuel Cafe brings in scones, bagels, and desserts (red velvet cake, carrot cake) from outside bakers. If you need a sugar fix, order a Pop-Tart. The cafe makes vegetarian soups and mostly vegetarian sandwiches, including peanut butter and jelly, spinach and provolone rollup, and a house specialty called the Buttafuoco: provolone, mozzarella, onions, tomatoes and Italian hot peppers on a sub roll.

CLIENTELE: The rare suburbanite who comes here usually gasps and quickly leaves. The crowd tends towards the young and countercultural, with a lot of students, artists, writers and photographers.

Half of all Americans over the age of 10 drink coffee.

GIL'S

2608 North Downer Avenue
Milwaukee, Wisconsin 53211 • (414) 964-4455
OPEN 8 A.M. TO 11 P.M. MONDAY TO THURSDAY;
8 A.M. TO MIDNIGHT FRIDAY; 9 A.M. TO MIDNIGHT SATURDAY;
9 A.M. TO 10:30 P.M. SUNDAY.

With a beer bar literally on every corner, Milwaukee really needed a place where non-drinkers could hang out. So in 1994 brothers Gil and Christopher Rasmussen opened Gil's, an elegant bilevel bistro with excellent food and entertainment. Located on city park land on the upscale Lower East Side, Gil's occupies a three-story, cream-colored brick building with screaming yellow awnings and large storefront windows. The interior is industrial-cozy, with exposed brick walls, wide plank pine floors, and huge steel ceiling beams. Downstairs there's a coffee bar and seating at imported Italian pine tables and rattan chairs. Go upstairs and you'll find a comfortable collection of '40s mohair couches, library tables and grade school chairs, as well as a counter where you can sit and watch the cooks work in the open kitchen. During the summer months, patrons spill out of the cafe onto the patio and park.

COFFEE: Gil's has a great selection of house specialties, made with coffee from local roaster Alterra. The cafe makes an enormous cappuccino, and serves iced mochas and cappuccinos by the pitcher (a popular concept in beer-crazy Milwaukee). Gil's also serves "smart drinks"—Chinese herbs, mixed with selzer or juice, that allegedly give your brain a kick start.

FOOD: The food, overseen by Gil himself (a graduate of New York's Culinary Institute of America in Hyde Park, New York), is wonderful. For breakfast there are muffins, authentic English scones and bagels, and on weekends, omelettes, oatmeal and quiche, as well as a theme brunch (Russian food, say, or Pennsylvania Dutch cuisine) on Sundays. Main meals feature soups, salads, sandwiches and pizza made with fresh dough. Try the Middle Eastern burrito, a Lebanese pita filled with hummus, baba ganoush, tabouli and tomatoes.

CLIENTELE: The crowd here is young, educated, and well-traveled.

LAVA JAVA

726 East Burleigh Street
Milwaukee, Wisconsin 53212 • (414) 265-5282
OPEN 7 A.M. TO 11 P.M. MONDAY TO THURSDAY;
7 A.M. TO MIDNIGHT FRIDAY; 9 A.M. TO MIDNIGHT SATURDAY;
9 A.M. TO 10 P.M. SUNDAY.

You'll see every conceivable type, from card-carrying NRA members to pierced punks, in this light, spacious coffeehouse in Milwaukee's River West district. Housed in a hundred-year-old brick storefront, it's divided into two sections, one smoking, the other non, plus a bookstore in back that sells books, cards and T-shirts. The high-ceilinged cafe is warm and inviting, with marble-topped tables, a volcano mural, and a skylight above the concrete and maple coffee bar. Outside, a fenced-in area has benches and tables. There are games (chess, backgammon, cards and cribbage), plus toys to keep the kiddies occupied.

COFFEE: The house blend is a Mocha Java from Equal Exchange, a company that promotes third-world coffee growers. The house specialty is the Butternut Latte, made with espresso, honey, hazelnut syrup, milk and a pat of butter (it's better than it sounds).

FOOD: The emphasis here is on vegetarian fare. Baked goods include bagels, muffins, cinnamon rolls, brownies, and cookies (the rainforest cookie with Brazil nuts and chocolate chips is a killer). Breakfast, served daily, features omelettes and hopple popple, made with chunks of potato, onion, egg, and cheese. Main courses include sandwiches, soups (spaghetti squash, vegetarian chili), and pizzas.

CLIENTELE: Lava Java attracts an eclectic crowd of conservative business people and students, artists and musicians.

CAFE WYRD

1600 West Lake Street
Minneapolis, Minnesota 55408 • (612) 827-5710
OPEN 7 A.M. TO 1 A.M. DAILY.

The nondescript facade of this cafe, with its blue awnings and discreetly lettered windows, is misleading, for it houses one of the hottest coffeehouses in Minneapolis. Located on the corner of Irving and Lake streets in the happening Uptown neighborhood, Cafe Wyrd (pronounced *weird)* is packed all the time, mostly with neighborhood regulars who appreciate its great food and whimsical, welcoming attitude. Open since 1991, it's proved so popular that owner Kim Bartmann recently took over the space next door and expanded. But it retains links with its humble beginnings—the staff still hand stamps all their to-go cups with the cafe's logo. Although the cafe caters to a wide range of customers, the area's large gay and lesbian population claims Cafe Wyrd as its own. In the summer in-line skaters, bicyclists and motorcyclists bop over from the city's famed Chain O'Lakes to sit and socialize on the patio.

COFFEE: Wyrd gets its coffee from local roaster B&W. Every day, it offers the Wyrd house blend plus a varietal that changes daily. Special drinks include the white mocha, made with melted Belgian white chocolate, and the dark mocha, made with Callebaut semi-sweet chocolate. For milk chocolate lovers, they make a Hershey's version.

FOOD: Chef Andy McQuigg makes everything from scratch, using mostly organic ingredients. For breakfast, there's awesome granola and a healthy fruit plate. At lunch, there's a homemade soup (try the yam-peanut-ginger or tomato basil) and several salads, such as pepper-Parmesan pasta and Shitake-peanut noodle. You can also order a bread and cheese plate, or antichoke dip and hummus. McQuigg makes fabulous muffins, pastries and desserts, including apple pie, carrot cake and fruit tarts.

CLIENTELE: About 80 percent of the cafe's clientele are regulars, including Generation Xers and well-heeled Uptown residents who live in nearby rehabbed Victorians.

AIMEE DuFRAIN, 22, financial analyst, Minneapolis: Coming to Minneapolis a few years ago from a small town, DuFrain, a lesbian, found that cafes, especially Cafe Wyrd, made her feel at home, and allowed her to meet other lesbians in a casual, unintimidating setting. "It's like a homing instinct to it. I heard about this cafe right away. It is just the place you go. If you have nothing else to do, you come here. It's my day off, and here I am."

FAVORITE DRINK: Double au lait. "I tried cappuccinos first. The foam was stupid."

PER DIEM: Just one.

CAFE STYLE: This is where she met her lover and where she comes to chat with friends. "It's so easy to get sucked into the banter; this is a really witty place."

HOW SHE BECAME AN ESPRESSO DRINKER: She comes from a town so small, the only exposure she ever got to the outside world was through public radio, until she ran into a group of espresso-drinking French exchange students. "They led me by the hand."

The half-life of caffeine in the body—the time it takes the body to get rid of half the caffeine consumed—is three to six hours.

Yam Peanut Ginger Soup
Cafe Wyrd, Minneapolis, Minnesota

2 large yams, peeled and coarsely chopped
1 medium potato, peeled and coarsely chopped
2 medium tomatoes, chopped
1 stalk celery
1 cinnamon stick
1/2 cup creamy peanut butter
2 tablespoons soy or canola oil
1 large onion, diced
2-inch cube fresh ginger, minced
1 teaspoon ground cumin seed
2 teaspoons ground coriander seed
1/8 teaspoon paprika
1/2 teaspoon ground chili pepper
pinch cayenne pepper (optional)
1/2 teaspoon Garam masala*
fresh cilantro for garnish
1/2 cup chopped roasted peanuts for garnish
salt to taste

1. Place chopped yams, potato, tomatoes, celery and cinnamon stick in a heavy pan and fill with enough water to cover. Bring to a boil, cover and reduce heat to a simmer until yams are very soft. Remove celery and cinnamon stick; add peanut butter to pot and stir to mix.
2. In small batches, puree the soup. (A blender makes the smoothest puree, but a food processor will work also.) You may need to add extra hot water to achieve a nice soup consistency.
3. In a skillet, saute the onion in the soy or canola oil until translucent. Add the ginger and saute two minutes, then stir in the spices and saute two more minutes.
4. Empty the skillet contents into the puree. Gently reheat and add salt to taste. Garnish each bowl with a sprinkle of chopped peanuts and a sprig of cilantro.

*Garam masala is a blend of roasted and ground spices that's available in Indian grocery stores and natural foods co-ops. If you can't find it, substitute a pinch of cloves, a pinch of nutmeg, and 1/8 teaspoon black pepper.

DUNN BROTHERS COFFEE

1569 Grand Avenue
St. Paul , Minnesota 55105 • (612) 698-0618
OPEN 6:30 A.M. TO 11 P.M. MONDAY TO THURSDAY;
6:30 A.M. TO MIDNIGHT FRIDAY;
7:30 A.M. TO MIDNIGHT SATURDAY; 7:30 A.M. TO 11 P.M. SUNDAY.

This bohemian student hangout, which opened in 1988, is practically an adjunct campus for Macalester College across the street. Located in an old brownstone commercial building that it shares with a kosher/vegetarian/Israeli restaurant, the cafe is dominated by an enormous roasting machine that runs all the time, filling the store with the heady aroma of fresh coffee. It's a crowded, noisy spot with 15 tables and benches (actually, old church pews painted green) along the walls. When it's crowded, customers share tables and strike up conversations with strangers.

COFFEE: Dunn Brothers is known for the strength of its coffee, figuring that customers who prefer a lighter brew can dilute it with hot water. They shun specialty cafe drinks with fancy names and serve only the basics: espresso, cappuccino, latte, etc.

FOOD: Because the cafe's emphasis is coffee, they don't serve food except for baked goods: breakfast pastries and light desserts supplied by outside vendors.

CLINETELE: The cafe draws students from Macalester College and residents from the Highland Park neighborhood. The crowd is understated and low key, not polished and upscale.

Latte *is Italian for* milk. *If you request a latte in Italy, you'll be served a glass of milk.*

KUPPERNICUS COFFEE GALLERY

308 Prince Street
St. Paul, Minnesota 55101 • (612) 290-2718
OPEN 7 A.M. TO 1 A.M. DAILY

This cafe helped jump-start a renaissance in the old warehouse district, where artists now live and work. Owner Nelson Paguyo took over the cavernous ground floor of an old railroad company warehouse in 1992 to create this unique coffeehouse. Floor-to-ceiling windows flood the space with light, and overhead are exposed wood beams. The 12,000-square-foot cafe looks like an enormous living room, with comfy couches, coffee tables, and La-Z-Boy recliners acquired at estate sales and secondhand furniture stores. (Regulars donated some of the pieces.) There's also an L-shaped bar with stools and a family-sized wood table and chairs, for those who balk at the unorthodox seating. On the walls hang art exhibits that change monthly. The space is so large and breathtaking that it's often used for weddings, company meetings and video shoots.

COFFEE: The coffee comes from local roaster B&W and includes a dark and medium roast daily. The house specialty is Thai coffee, very sweet and made from a secret recipe.

FOOD: The cafe brings in pastries from an outside vendor. No other food is served.

CLIENTELE: About 90 percent of Kuppernicus' customers are artists who live and work nearby. The rest are tourists who come to gawk at the enormity of it all.

Coffee is the primary export crop of more than 60 countries.

MUDDY WATERS

2401 Lyndale Avenue South
Minneapolis, Minnesota 55405 • (612) 872-2232
OPEN 7 A.M. TO 1 A.M. MONDAY TO FRIDAY;
8 A.M. TO 1 A.M. SATURDAY AND SUNDAY.

This kitsch palace on Minneapolis' south side proves that you can go home again—that is, if home was suburbia, circa 1970. With a wacky menu that features Pop-Tarts, Spaghetti-Os, Campbell's soup and Rice Krispies bars, this is the place for Baby Boomers and Generation Xers looking for a blast from their past. Co-owners Kristi Berkvam and Gail Sullivan opened Muddy Waters in 1989 in an old brick building, outfitting it with '50s chrome tables and chairs and weird fluorescent lights covered with pink tubing.

COFFEE: The coffee comes from the local European Roastery. You can also get freshly squeezed juices.

FOOD: The food is cheap and most of it comes from a can or a box. But for fresh food fanatics, there's the peanut butter and jelly sandwich, served with a side of Bugles corn chips.

CLIENTELE: This used to be strictly a neighborhood joint, attracting young locals and business people on their way to work. But outsiders, especially tourists, have discovered this wacky place.

The cast and crew of ABC's Ellen *go through 20 pounds of Kona, 5 pounds of decaf, 2 to 3 pounds of vanilla-macadamia nut and 1 pound of espresso each week.*

BEST COFFEEHOUSES IN THE...

SOUTH/ SOUTHWEST

METRO AREAS

Albuquerque
Austin
Dallas–Ft. Worth
Houston
Memphis
New Orleans
Santa Fe
Tucson

DOUBLE RAINBOW BAKERY CAFE

3416 Central Avenue S.E.
Albuquerque, New Mexico 87106 • (505) 255-6633
OPEN 6:30 A.M. TO MIDNIGHT DAILY.

This small but enchanting brick-fronted cafe is sandwiched between two bookstores on the street that was once called Route 66. Located in the hip Nob Hill section of Albuquerque, Double Rainbow does triple duty, serving as a coffeehouse, newsstand, and full bakery. The decor is minimalist: old tile floors, green walls, pastry cases crammed with home-made goodies, and a functional-looking counter of stainless steel and Formica underneath a 25-foot skywell. Forty feet of magazine racks display an extensive selection of papers and magazines for sale, and nobody seems to mind customers who read and don't buy. Place your order at the counter, then proceed up a short flight of stairs to the dining area, illuminated by a second soaring skylight, where an employee will bring you your food.

COFFEE: The coffee here, from local roaster Norm Whiting, is high quality and basic—no flavorings or syrups. There's a house blend and a decaf, plus the standard espresso drinks, all served in glass mugs.

FOOD: Everything here is baked from scratch on the premises, including Danish, coffee cake, bagels, breads and croissants. For lunch there are sandwiches, served on homemade bread, and a couple of hot entrees, such as chicken pot pie and lasagna. Dessert runs the gamut from fancy European tortes and truffle cakes to old-fashioned American favorites such as coconut cream pie. On the weekends, Double Rainbow serves a full breakfast menu.

CLIENTELE: The cafe is crowded with University of New Mexico students, pilots from nearby Kirkland Air Force Base, and local business people, doctors and lawyers.

FRED'S BREADS & BAGELS

3009 Central Avenue N.E.
Albuquerque, New Mexico 87106 • (505) 266-7323
OPEN 6:30 A.M. TO 6 P.M. DAILY.

Although it's only been around since 1991, Fred's is an Albuquerque institution: laid-back, unpretentious, with an old-fashioned coffeehouse personality that has made it a favorite with University of New Mexico students. The exterior is all glass and big wooden doors, with a large neon toaster sign in the window and a few plastic chairs on the sidewalk. The funky interior features old red vinyl booths (very cool) and mismatched wood tables and chairs, where you can sit and watch the bakers work in the exposed kitchen. The concrete walls feature enormous murals of Frank Zappa and James Brown, plus signed and framed photos of musicians who've hung out here: Phish, Wynton Marsalis, the Meat Puppets, to name a few.

COFFEE: Fred's, which gets its coffee from local Santa Fe Coffee Roasters, serves a house blend, a decaf, and a French roast with chicory. (Refills are free.) The espresso drinks are the old standards of flavored and unflavored lattes, mochas, etc.

FOOD: The kitchen turns out excellent (and oversized) muffins, scones, croissants, Danish, cinnamon rolls and sticky buns, as well as bagels. For lunch you can order deli and vegetarian sandwiches.

CLIENTELE: Local business people, lawyers, architects, and doctors from nearby Carolinas Medical Center come for their morning fix.

JAVA JOE'S

906 Park Avenue S.W.
Albuquerque, New Mexico 87102 • (505) 764-9999
OPEN 7 A.M. TO 4 P.M. DAILY.

Located between downtown and touristy Old Town, this bustling coffeehouse is so popular on weekends that the crowd literally spills out onto the sidewalk, and patrons grab a seat wherever they can find one: on the curb, the ground, or a nearby parked car. Java Joe's faux-adobe exterior is adorned with arresting graffiti murals, while the inside is open and airy, with mint green walls, changing art exhibits, and lots of greenery. The pace is hectic at lunch but slows down in the late afternoon, a good time to come in and peruse at your leisure the magazines and newspapers left out for customers to read. Kids are welcome, too: there's a stack of children's books to amuse them.

COFFEE: Java Joe's offers an excellent house blend from Allegro, and refills are free; serve yourself from an air pot on the counter. The lattes are served in large ceramic mugs.

FOOD: In addition to homemade pastries such as scones, muffins, croissants and coffee cakes, Java Joe's serves waffles, oatmeal, granola, breakfast burritos and bagel combos such as the Europa, a toasted bagel topped with roasted red peppers, grilled onions, garlic-flavored olive oil, and smoked Gruyere. For lunch, you'll find soups (green chile chowder is a favorite), salads and deli sandwiches. Finish off your meal with a scoop of Double Rainbow ice cream or sorbet.

CLIENTELE: Java Joe pulls in both the downtown and Old Town crowds, including attorneys and architects, students, artists and young families who live nearby.

CAPTAIN QUACKENBUSH'S ESPRESSO CAFE

2120 Guadalupe Street
Austin, Texas 78705 • (512) 472-4477
OPEN 7 A.M. TO MIDNIGHT MONDAY TO FRIDAY;
8 A.M. TO MIDNIGHT SATURDAY AND SUNDAY.

Captain Quackenbush's is the venerable granddad of coffeehouses in a town full of upstarts. Opened in 1983 by an ex-Berkeley resident named Art Silver, it introduced California coffee culture to Austin and was featured in the film *Slackers*. There are those who say it ain't what it used to be, but Quackenbush's still knows how to draw a crowd. It's divided into a cafe with seating for 100 and a gift shop where you can buy cards, posters, coffee by the pound and comic books. Order your coffee at the counter and sit down inside or at the open-air patio in front. The staff is friendly and the atmosphere relaxed; you're likely to find a professor from the University of Texas, which is just across the street, holding class here. On Friday and Saturday nights waddle upstairs to Quack's Up, for live jazz and blues music from 9 p.m. to 2 a.m.

COFFEE: Quackenbush's considers itself an espresso bar, so the emphasis here is on the strong stuff. The secret blend comes from Schapira Coffee and Tea, a New York roaster. If you're very brave you'll try the house specialty, Leo's Crowbar: a quadruple espresso with a splash of milk. ("It's better than sex or Prozac," Silver promises.)

FOOD: The cafe serves light meals: breakfast tacos and pastries, vegetarian chili, spinach casserole, and soups, salads and sandwiches. Everything is made in Quackenbush's kitchen on the premises.

CLIENTELE: This is mostly a University of Texas student gathering spot.

MATTHEW FEINER, 28, artist and university student, Austin, Texas:

Cafes are the critical social institution in Feiner's life. Not only does he drink on average, believe it or not, 14 shots of espresso a day, but his artwork has found an appreciative home on the walls of numerous cafes in the last two years. A multimedia artist, Feiner makes "socio-political" collages about societal apathy toward poverty, war and AIDS, and he finds cafe audiences refreshingly receptive and encouraging.

Favorite drink: Double macchiato. That's two shots of espresso and a drop of milk. He switched from cappuccinos when he realized he was lactose-intolerant.

Per diem: Seven double macchiatos. "It gets me going, that's for sure. I'll have two or three at a sitting."

Favorite cafe: Captain Quackenbush's Espresso Cafe, across the street from the University of Texas.

Cafes as art galleries: "In cafes, you'll see a much better cross section of new art, a good representation of talented, young, often raw art styles that you won't see in a museum or a gallery."

Why he likes his work in cafes: "The 'people' are there. My art gets seen. People can sit and talk about the art. I had my work in galleries in New York, but there were no people there. In a cafe I get better feedback, encouragement, and better sales."

METRO ESPRESSO BAR

2222 B Guadalupe Street
Austin, Texas 78705 • (512) 474-5730
OPEN 24 HOURS A DAY, SEVEN DAYS A WEEK.

The name says it all: Metro comes alive at 10 p.m. and doesn't wind down until the wee hours. Austin, home to the University of Texas and known for its high quotient of slackers, is the perfect location for this California-grown coffee bar. Founded by a couple of University of California-Berkeley school chums, it has a post-modern industrial look and a laid-back, welcoming atmosphere. Located on the Drag directly across from University of Texas' west gate, Metro resides in an old vaudeville theater. The two-story interior has an old cement floor, brick walls, and stainless steel wainscoting and counters. Huge menu stands soar 14 feet into the air, requiring customers to throw their heads way back to see what's available. The tables and chairs are quirky three-legged metal sculptures that look great (but your body won't tolerate sitting on them for more than an hour or so). Upstairs, there's mezzanine seating with a great view of the University of Texas campus and clock tower.

COFFEE: The coffee comes from Espresso Roma, a Berkeley, California roastery. Metro prides itself on being able to make anything the customer wants, including flavored espresso drinks and iced coffee drinks served from jet spray machines. Specials include the Hammerhead, a large coffee with two shots of espresso, and the Depth Charge, coffee with one espresso shot. Metro also serves milkshakes, Coke shakes, and espresso shakes, such as the Espresso Rocket Shake: chocolate ice cream, a banana, espresso and skim milk.

FOOD: The kitchen makes breakfast pastries, including apple cinnamon muffins, double chocolate chip muffins, and mocha scones. They also carry croissants, bagels, cookies and cakes from outside suppliers. For lunch, there are healthy sandwiches from a local vendor.

CLIENTELE: Undergraduate students from University of Texas have made this their home away from home. In the morning, people from the Scientology building next door come in for their daily fix. Metro really gets packed when the local bars close at 2 a.m.

Mocha Scones
Metro Espresso Bar, Austin, Texas

- 4 cups flour
- 4 teaspoons baking powder
- 1/2 cup sugar
- 1/3 cup cocoa powder
- 2 tablespoons ground espresso beans
- 1/4 pound butter
- 2 cups sour cream
- 1 teaspoon almond extract

1. Preheat oven to 325°F.
2. In a large bowl, sift together flour, baking powder and sugar. Add cocoa powder and ground espresso beans to flour mixture.
3. Using a pastry cutter or your fingers, cut butter into flour mixture until it resembles small crumbs.
4. Mix sour cream and almond extract together, then add to flour-butter mixture. Mix lightly until dough holds together.
5. Form dough into a ball, flatten slightly, then cut into eight wedges. Place scones on a greased cookie sheet and bake 15 to 20 minutes until done.

Coffee is the world's second largest traded commodity after oil.

LITTLE CITY ESPRESSO BAR AND CAFE

916 Congress Avenue
Austin, Texas 78701 • (512) 476-2489
OPEN 8 A.M. TO MIDNIGHT MONDAY TO THURSDAY;
8 A.M. TO 1 A.M. FRIDAY; 9 A.M. TO 1 A.M. SATURDAY;
9 A.M. TO 10 P.M. SUNDAY.

Voted Austin's best coffeehouse in 1994 by the readers of the alternative newspaper, *The Chronicle,* Little City is known for its friendly staff and its funky decor. Located in a landmark building downtown near the State Capitol, it has rough, distressed walls hung with changing art and a flaking metal billboard from the '50s. The tables are cement, the chairs wood covered with brown canvas. Little City seats only 52, but has high ceilings and a spacious feel—although when the place gets busy the line at the counter stretches all the way to the back of the shop. A large menu hangs from the ceiling behind the counter, and mellow jazz and blues—Cab Calloway, Ella Fitzgerald—play on the sound system.

COFFEE: The coffee comes from La Creme, a Dallas roaster, and includes the house blend, a decaf, and a flavor that changes daily. Little City uses the Italian method of making espresso drinks: short pulls, no foam. The house specialty is the Funky Monkey: a double cafe mocha with banana flavoring.

FOOD: In the morning there are breakfast pastries from outside vendors. Lunch includes soups (try the garlicky basil-tomato), salads and sandwiches, such as the roast turkey with basil pesto and sun-dried cranberries. Desserts include cheesecake flan, Frangelico cupcakes, and the salty oat cookie, an oatmeal cookie topped with salt that the regulars swear by.

CLIENTELE: The clientele ranges from Bubbas to socialites from the upscale Highland Park and University Park neighborhoods. It also includes a hefty dose of students, faculty and staff from Southern Methodist University.

RUTA MAYA COFFEE COMPANY

218 West Fourth Street
Austin, Texas 78701 • (512) 472-9637
OPEN 7 A.M. TO 2 A.M. DAILY.

Regular patrons of this quirky coffeehouse in Austin's West End (the old warehouse district) revel in the way it combines politically correct and incorrect notions. In PC fashion, it celebrates Latin American culture and kicks back a portion of its profits to a foundation that preserves Central American ruins, yet it unapologetically sets aside a smoking lounge where Bubbas can indulge in cigars and air their contrarian views. Ruta Maya began as a coffee wholesaler, roasting coffee grown by small Mexican cooperatives and distributing it to local grocery stores and restaurants. The cafe opened in 1993 in two-story red brick warehouse building, with 14-foot ceilings, wood floors and indoor seating for about 60. The walls are covered with Mexican tapestries and photos, and local artists display their work behind a stage. All day long the air is perfumed with the smell of coffee roasting in a huge Diedrich machine in the cafe. A separate room houses the smoking lounge, where customers can buy and smoke premium and super-premium cigars (brands include Macanudo, Avo and Partagas; occasionally you can even purchase contra band Cuban cigars) and imported cigarettes. The best seats in the house are actually outside: A former loading dock serves as the patio, with seating for about 65.

COFFEE: Ruta Maya roasts about 15 varieties on the premises and offers a choice of light, medium and dark roasts. The espresso drinks are standard—no flavorings available. Try the Mexican coffee from Chiapas; it's smooth and delicious.

FOOD: The menu is simple: breakfast burritos and bagels in the morning, pre-made sandwiches for lunch. The baked goods, all made off the premises, include pecan pie, coffee liqueur pie, and macrobiotic cookies.

CLIENTELE: In the morning local architects, bankers and lawyers stop in for their daily caffeine. Ruta Maya also attracts students from the University of Texas and people interested in the Latin American scene.

AROMAS COFFEE

5409 Beltline Road
Dallas, Texas 75240 • (214) 980-1116
OPEN 7 A.M. TO 10:30 P.M. MONDAY TO THRUSDAY; 7 A.M. TO MIDNIGHT FIRDAY; 8 A.M. TO MIDNIGHT SATURDAY; 10 A.M. TO 10:30 P.M. SUNDAY.

Don't let its location in a nondescript strip mall fool you. This bustling coffeehouse is the hip place to go in North Dallas after dinner or the movies. The decor is simple: grey textured walls, tile floors and comfy wooden chairs and tables. But the coffee is rich and complex. It comes from Caravelli, the Washington state roaster that recently acquired the five-store Aromas chain.

COFFEE: Buy it in bulk or in a cup. You'll find more than 40 different beans, all listed on a big menu board. Each day Aromas offers five brews, which it rotates from its stock. There's also the usual espresso drinks: latte, cappuccino, mocha, plus flavored specialties like espresso milk-shakes and the Razzmatazz (raspberry mocha).

FOOD: Aromas brings in great desserts from local bakers, including chocolate cake, cheesecake, pecan pie, plus scones, muffins, and cinnamon rolls. Don't miss the to-die-for Mile-High Carrot Cake.

CLIENTELE: The crowd here ranges in age from 20 to 40, mostly young professionals and people looking for a place to discuss the movie they just saw at the theater next door.

According to a study by Johns Hopkins University, caffeine is an addictive substance.

DEEP JAVA

2639-C Elm Street

Dallas, Texas 75226 • (214) 742-5282

OPEN 8 A.M. TO MIDNIGHT TUESDAY TO THURSDAY;
8 A.M. TO 3:30 A.M. FRIDAY, NOON TO 3:30 A.M. SATURDAY;
NOON TO 9 P.M. SUNDAY. CLOSED MONDAY.

Deep Java introduced Dallas to the coffeehouse concept when it opened in 1992. With its mismatched, beat-up old furniture, changing art display and Wednesday night poetry readings, it's the archetypal coffee hangout. In fact, the *Dallas Morning News* in 1994 rated it the coffeehouse with the best atmosphere. Located in a section of town called Deep Ellum, which was once filled with deserted manufacturing facilties and warehouses, the area is vibrantly alive with art galleries, clubs and restaurants, Deep Java attracts a wide cross section of Dallas residents, from business types to the young art crowd. The interior is dark, with old concrete floors and a stairway leading to a small loft, where patrons can smoke and thumb through an assortment of old books.

COFFEE: Deep Java gets its beans from Country Coffee, a roaster in Tyler, Texas. It offers five blends a day and basic espresso drinks. The house specialty is frozen cappuccino.

FOOD: Breakfast includes omelettes, bacon and eggs, turkey monsieur, and breakfast tacos. For lunch, try the Greek pizza, with feta cheese, artichoke hearts, black olives, Roma tomatoes, and mozzarella and parmesan cheeses. Sandwiches, salads, soups and baked potatoes are also available.

CLIENTELE: The suit-and-tie crowd drops by for coffee on their way downtown to work. In the evening, the clientele is considerably younger, mostly people on their way to or from the area's clubs, bars, restaurants and movie theaters.

THE COFFEE HAUS

404 Houston Street
Fort Worth, Texas 76102 • (817) 336-5282
OPEN 8 A.M. TO 11 P.M. SUNDAY TO THURSDAY;
8 A.M. TO MIDNIGHT FRIDAY AND SATURDAY.

This handsome downtown cafe is a cosmopolitan stomping ground for Fort Worth coffee lovers. Out front there's seating at wrought-iron tables under a beautiful copper awning. Inside, the design is cool and contemporary, with dark-grey tiled floor and countertops and a maple, raised-panel bar. Another bar runs along the windowed storefront, where patrons can sit and watch the foot traffic as they drink cappuccino made in an imposing black and brass domed espresso machine. Coffee beans are displayed in glass-fronted brass silos on one wall, beneath an unusual topographic map of the world's coffee-growing regions. Another wall features a neon sculpture of a steaming cup of coffee.

COFFEE: The coffee is roasted, blended and flavored by Coffee Haus' owner Don Noe at his Arlington, Texas store. The shop offers a daily choice of light, dark, flavored and decaf, as well as espresso drinks. The mochas and cappuccinos are served in big bowls. The Coffee Haus is known for the House Cap, a sweet version of cappuccino made with light-roasted espresso and vanilla syrup.

FOOD: You'll find an extensive selection of pastries and desserts, made by outside bakers, including bagels, scones, croissants, muffins, Key lime pie and cakes: blackout chocolate, carrot, German chocolate, and Italian cream. For lunch, you can order simple soups and sandwiches.

CLIENTELE: The Coffee Haus' downtown location draws a lot of business people during the day. Later, it fills with students from Texas Christian University and people from nearby museums, jazz clubs, art galleries, and an 11-screen movie theater.

ROCK-N-JAVA

2906 North Henderson Avenue
Dallas, Texas 75206 • (214) 827-5282

OPEN 6:30 A.M. TO MIDNIGHT SUNDAY TO THURSDAY; 6:30 A.M. TO 3 A.M. (AND SOMETIMES LATER) FRIDAY AND SATURDAY.

When this attractive cafe opened in late 1994, it was a shocker to staid Dallasites. Modeled on a bordello, it has big overstuffed couches and chairs, antique end tables and lamps, gilt-framed mirrors, distressed walls and a red glazed ceiling. The enormous velvet-clad furniture has an *Alice in Wonderland* air that invites you to sink down and make yourself at home. Located across the highway from ritzy Highland Park in an area filled with antique shops, art galleries and restaurants, Rock-N-Java is housed in a turn-of-the-century bow-front brick building with lots of windows and a neon sign out front. There's an outdoor patio on the side with seating for about 20. Coffee is served in elegant black ceramic bowls.

COFFEE: A local roaster prepares the beans. There are five brews available daily—a house blend, a flavored brew, house and flavored decaf and a roast of the day. In addition to the basic espresso drinks, you can order fabulous blended iced mochas or the Sledgehammer: four shots of espresso mixed with half and half.

FOOD: A light breakfast menu includes steamed eggs made in the espresso machine, breakfast burrito, oatmeal, granola, and breakfast pastries. The lunch menu consists of submarine sandwiches, such as the Italian—lettuce, tomato, onion, provolone, salami and ham.

CLIENTELE: Local business people, artist types, college students and gays populate this cafe. The crowd is trendy, not grungy.

CAFE MAISON COFFEE ROASTERY & ESPRESSO BAR

2089 Westheimer Road
Houston, Texas 77098 • (713) 528-6750
OPEN 7 A.M. TO 10 P.M. SUNDAY TO WEDNESDAY;
7 A.M. TO MIDNIGHT THURSDAY TO SATURDAY.

Extremely personal service is the hallmark of this coffeehouse, which uses two unusual mini roasting machines to do small-batch roasting. Located in a brick strip mall in the upscale Upper Kirby shopping district of Houston, Cafe Maison has a faux marble wall and red mahogany shelves that display bulk coffees, teas, cocoas and coffeemaking accoutrements. Marble-topped tables and barstools provide seating for about 30. On a pedestal in the center of the shop stand two stainless steel Nu-vu mini roasters, where workers custom roast as little as a half pound of bulk coffee to order. At the two coffee bars, you can order from an array of specialty coffee drinks, such as the Cafe Snicker, a chocolate-peanut latte.

COFFEE: The coffee here is high quality and super fresh—nothing is older than a couple of days. The coffee menu lists five brews and 70 espresso drinks, including the Caramello (caramel cappuccino topped with whipped cream and drizzled with warm caramel sauce) and the Cocoa Mocha (cinnamon hazelnut praline cocoa with a shot of espresso, topped with whipped cream and chocolate flakes). Cafe Maison also offers French press coffees and teas, iced coffees, granitas and milkshakes. Try the Turkey Cold Cooler: chocolate ice cream, Kahlua flavoring, coffee and Coke topped with whipped cream and chocolate flakes.

FOOD: The fare is light and simple: two kinds of quiche, large cheese-stuffed croissants, and homemade jumbo muffins, including lemon poppyseed, cranberry orange, apple spice and lemon-blueberry. The cafe also serves cakes, cheesecake, lemon bars, chocolate-raspberry brownies and bread pudding from an outside supplier.

CLIENTELE: Local politicians, business folks, and college students from nearby Rice University and the University of St. Thomas come for great coffee.

CYRANO'S COFFEE ROASTERY & CAFE

4100 Montrose Boulevard
Houston, Texas 77006 • (713) 523-7787
OPEN 11 A.M. TO 7 P.M. SUNDAY TO THURSDAY;
11 A.M. TO MIDNIGHT FRIDAY AND SATURDAY.

The building that houses this coffeehouse was once a church, and the owners have kept many of the original features, including the stained glass and belltower. The brightly lit space in Houston's Montrose area (near the Houston Medical Center and museums) is divided into a retail shop, complete with a roaster, and a cafe with booths, tables, and a long marble counter and ice cream parlor stools. A menu board lists 20 to 30 brewed coffees daily, but if you don't see what you want, you can choose one of the 70 varietals sold in the retail store—a staffer will fetch the beans and grind them to order. Outside, there's a covered patio and seating on the front sidewalk.

COFFEE: Brewed coffee is a religion at this church-turned-cafe, where staffers grind and prepare each order individually and serve the coffee in a two-cup carafe. Although espresso drinks are available, the emphasis is on brewed coffees.

FOOD: Cyrano's serves light lunch fare, Ben & Jerry's ice creams, and desserts from outside suppliers. (Try the exquisite Salzburg chocolate cake.) They also bake their own cookies and brownies. For more substantial fare, you can eat next door at the Black Labrador Pub.

CLIENTELE: Cyrano's draws on several nearby colleges, including Rice, St. Thomas, Texas Southern University and the University of Houston, as well as the renowned High School of Visual and Performing Arts. Montrose's large art community and academic types from Houston Medical Center are also represented here.

There are 200,000 coffee bars in Italy.

DOLCE & FREDDO

5515 Kirby Drive
Houston, Texas 77005 • (713) 521-3260
OPEN 11 A.M. TO MIDNIGHT SUNDAY TO THURSDAY;
11 A.M. TO 1 A.M. FRIDAY AND SATURDAY.

This upscale spot is a contemporary fantasy of an Italian cafe: bright, spare and inviting. The owners of Dolce & Freddo (Italian for sweet and cold) spared no expense in creating this spectacular dessert shop in Houston's villagey West University neighborhood. Red awnings cover the windows, and red neon runs around the building's perimeter. A big deck on the sidewalk out front has about 15 tables and umbrellas. Inside, there are granite-topped tables, a long, modern bar of wood, granite and stainless steel, topped with curved glass display cases filled with cakes, pastries, and homemade gelatos and sorbettos. Behind that is a back bar, where coffees and liqueurs are displayed on mirrored glass shelves. Order any coffee drink you like; there's no menu to hamper your imagination. Prices here are high, but the drinks are worth every penny.

COFFEE: The coffee comes from Illycaffe, a pricey brand that many consider the world's best. American coffee here is made to order; it's actually espresso diluted with hot water. There isn't a coffee drink menu to consult, but the cappuccino is excellent. The cafe also carries liqueurs, Italian beers and wines, brandies and cognacs.

FOOD: Dolce & Freddo started out as a gelateria, and it's still known for its wonderfully rich Italian ices and creams, made fresh on the premises every day. You'll also find European biscotti and pastries, including Italian cream cake and Black Forest cake. No other food is served.

CLIENTELE: Homesick foreigners come here for a fix of European atmosphere. Dolce & Freddo also attracts families, couples and upscale business executives.

COFFEE CELLAR

3573 Southern Avenue

Memphis, Tennessee 38111 • (901) 320-7853

OPEN 7 A.M. TO MIDNIGHT MONDAY TO FRIDAY; 8 A.M. TO MIDNIGHT SATURDAY; 9 A.M. TO 8 P.M. SUNDAY.

This funky college hangout across the railroad tracks from the University of Memphis has a cheerful yellow exterior and a comforting, laid-back presence. The coffeehouse has two levels: up front there's a small smoking area with a handful of seats, and down a small flight of stairs is the "cellar," a larger room with a 20-foot-long coffee bar, Formica tables and comfy dark leather armchairs. The decor is French country funk, with walls sponge-painted yellow and red and an unusual painted-plywood floor. Friendly, Southern-accented employees will take your order at the counter, then deliver it to you at a table. In the summer, there's seating out front at two small tables.

COFFEE: The Coffee Gallery of Memphis supplies the coffee, and there are always three brews on tap: regular, flavored and decaf. The first refill is free; every refill thereafter costs 25 cents. There's an extensive espresso drink menu; favorites include the Thunderthighs (espresso with steamed cream, sugar, chocolate, oil of almond and ground Ghirardelli milk chocolate) and Caffe Franklin (steamed sweetened condensed milk, espresso and cinnamon). The Cellar also carries Snapple, teas, juice and soda.

FOOD: There's a full line of pastries made on the premises, including cinnamon rolls, croissants, cream cheese Danish and muffins. (Try the kitchen sink muffin, made with molasses, walnuts, carrots, raisins and coconut.) The lunch menu features soups, salads and sandwiches, such as walnut-tuna or dilled chicken salad. The rollups are popular: a 10-inch flour tortilla with cream cheese, fresh spinach, tomatoes, and meat and cheese (roast beef and jack, for example). For dessert, try the caramel fudge pecan cake, the black and white espresso cake, or the hazelnut puzzle cake.

CLIENTELE: Local business folk and University of Memphis students come to eat and socialize.

THE COFFEE GALLERY

7820 Poplar Avenue
Germantown, Tennessee 38138 • (901) 754-1123
OPEN 7 A.M. TO 9 P.M. MONDAY TO THURSDAY;
7 A.M. TO 10 P.M. FRIDAY AND SATURDAY;
11 A.M. TO 6 P.M. SUNDAY.

Three walls of glass give this friendly coffeehouse/roastery a sense of light and openness. Located in a strip mall in a small residential suburb adjacent to Memphis, the Coffee Gallery caters to an affluent neighborhood clientele. Outside, cafe tables fill a grassy area; inside there's seating for 40 at cloth-covered tables (and every seat has a window view). The walls are lined with shelves holding coffee-related items and European gourmet foods, and in the back of the shop a roaster is partly visible. Four menu boards offer coffee, sandwiches and frozen yogurt; place your order and pick up at the counter.

COFFEE: Coffee Gallery roasts its own coffee and offers four brews every day. In addition to the full line of espresso drinks, there are house specialties such as the Cappuccino Thrill (espresso blended with vanilla yogurt and ice) and the Iced Banana Raspberry dream (espresso, cold milk, chocolate and raspberry flavorings and ice, topped with whipped cream and a dash of chocolate).

FOOD: There's a yogurt bar, offering six flavors of Colombo non-fat frozen yogurt and 20 toppings, and a deli where you can get bagels and pastries, made on the premises, and soup, salad and sandwiches, including the Monet (turkey, ham and cheddar) and the Gallery (warm turkey, crispy bacon and melted provolone cheese, served with a pickle and potato salad).

CLIENTELE: This is a middle-of-the-road crowd of working people and local residents who bring the kids in with them.

CAFE DU MONDE

800 Decatur Street
New Orleans, Louisiana 70116 • (504) 525-4544
OPEN 24 HOURS A DAY (CLOSED CHRISTMAS DAY).

Cafe du Monde may be the most celebrated coffeehouse in the country, beloved by tourists and locals alike for its simple menu—creamy cafe au lait and beignets—and its long, rich history. Located across the street from Jackson Square in New Orleans' historic French Quarter, it got its start in the mid-19th century as a coffee stand (actually, just a wooden barrel with a coffee pot on top), where vendors from the bustling city marketplace came for their daily jolt of java. In the 1940s, the cafe, which by then was housed in an old marketplace building, was bought by the Fernandez family, who run it to this day. The interior is tiny—just 19 tables—but the outdoor patio seats 400. There, under slowly turning ceiling fans, waiters rush by with trays of coffee and pastry.

COFFEE: There's virtually no choice here, just cafe au lait (half coffee, half steamed milk). A couple of years ago, Cafe du Monde broke tradition to serve iced cafe au lait, a big hit in a town where the temperature regularly tops 100. If you must be different, you can also order decaf coffee, fresh squeezed orange juice, milk or chocolate milk.

FOOD: The only food available here are beignets, lovely lumps of fried dough, liberally dusted with powdered sugar, that emit clouds of steam when pulled apart. They are practically synonymous with New Orleans and Cafe du Monde.

WARNING: Avoid Cafe du Monde during Mardi Gras, unless you enjoy gulping down your coffee while surrounded by hordes of drunken revelers.

CLIENTELE: Tourists abound, of course, but locals also swear by the place. Families, high-schoolers on prom night, Mardi Gras revelers in gowns and tuxedos—they're all here.

CAFFE! CAFFE!

4301 Clearview Parkway
Metairie, Louisiana 70006 • (504) 885-4845
OPEN 7 A.M. TO 11 P.M. MONDAY TO THURSDAY;
7 A.M. TO MIDNIGHT FRIDAY; 8 A.M. TO MIDNIGHT SATURDAY;
8 A.M. TO 10 P.M. SUNDAY.

This bright, contemporary cafe in the affluent New Orleans suburb of Metairie attracts an upscale mix of professional people and local housewives. Located on the corner of Clearview and West Esplanade in a slate-blue brick building with large glass doors and a hot pink neon sign, Caffe! Caffe! is a pleasant spot to while away an hour. The interior is colorful, with slate-blue tables, a pickled wood counter with a brass espresso machine, and walls papered in a muted wash of pastel colors. Customers make their choices from a large menu board on the back wall, then line up at the pastry case to order. Outside, there's a sidewalk deck with wrought iron tables and chairs, as well as umbrellas to shade patrons from the brutal New Orleans sun. Try the coffee with chicory, a New Orleans oddity that dates from the Civil War, when coffee was so expensive it was mixed with the ground root of the chicory plant. Chicory's strong taste isn't for everyone, but locals swear it's great for the digestive system.

COFFEE: Caffe! Caffe!, which gets its coffee from several roasters, offers a medium and dark roast, two decafs, and a flavored blend every day. The house specialty is Caffe Royale, made with hot chocolate, expresso and whipped cream. They also offer iced coffees and Nectar and Italian sodas. Buy the $2.75 travel mug and Caffe! Caffe! will rinse it out and refill it at a special price when you bring it in.

FOOD: Breakfast is limited to croissants, muffins and other morning pastries. Lunch, served from 11 a.m. to 8 p.m., includes homemade soups, salads and sandwiches. They're known for their chicken salad (fresh chunks of breast meat with mayonnaise, celery and walnuts) and the grilled Caesar pita (a soft pita folded over grilled chicken and Caesar salad). The desserts, made on the premises, include creme brulee, pound cake, and white chocolate bread pudding.

CLIENTELE: This is an older, more affluent crowd than many coffeehouses attract: neighborhood moms who come for coffee and chat after dropping the kids off at school, business people holding meetings, doctors and nurses.

The patent for the first espresso machine was granted in 1910.

PJ'S COFFEE & TEA CO.

7624 Maple Street
New Orleans, Louisiana 70118 • (504) 486-2827
OPEN 7 A.M. TO 11 P.M. MONDAY TO FRIDAY;
8 A.M. TO 11 P.M. SATURDAY AND SUNDAY.

In 1978 Phyllis Jordan, a social worker, was looking to make a career change when she opened the first in what became a successful chain of 15 coffeehouses in New Orleans. The Maple Street mothership, located in a neighborhood that adjoins both Tulane and Loyola universities, began as a small retail store selling coffee, tea and their paraphernalia. When Jordan added some tables and chairs two years later, the business really took off. PJ's is devoted to the art of conversation and coffee, so you won't find too many distractions here. The menu is limited to pastries that complement the coffee, and the atmosphere is low key and unobtrusive. The soothing salmon-pink walls are hung with coffee-related artwork, and classical and jazz music play softly in the background. The spacious interior seats about 100 at Formica-topped tables and small wooden chairs. The cafe's dominant feature is the view through French doors of the patio. There, a fountain burbles and light dapples through overhead rafters.

COFFEE: PJ's roasts its own coffee seven days a week at an off-site facility. The cafe serves a medium roast, a dark roast and a decaf, but no flavored coffees. The specialty is the Vienna cream, a combination of coffee concentrate, milk, sugar and froth that tastes like a hot ice cream. In 1980 PJ's started the local craze for iced coffee, which used to be dismissed here as a "Yankee drink."

FOOD: The cafe offers a wide array of pastries, made by outside suppliers, that complement the coffee. Most popular: a rich chocolate buttercream square.

CLIENTELE: Rich kids from Tulane's fraternities and sororities come here to meet and occasionally study. PJ's also gets a mixed crowd of young families, local professionals, and black-T-shirted high-schoolers.

RUE DE LA COURSE

1500 Magazine Street
New Orleans, Louisiana 70130 • (504) 529-1455
OPEN 7 A.M. TO 11 P.M. MONDAY TO THURSDAY;
7 A.M. TO MIDNIGHT FRIDAY; 8 A.M. TO MIDNIGHT SATURDAY;
8 A.M. TO 11 P.M. SUNDAY.

This shop, open since 1990, has more than a dash of theatricality. Co-owner Debra Dunn, who once worked as a visual director for Esprit, modeled it after traditional London coffeehouses of the 16th and 17th centuries. It's located on the corner of Magazine and Race Streets (hence the name Rue de la Course, which is French for Race Street) in one of the Greek Revival-style brick buildings that abound in New Orleans' historic Lower Garden District. With its old painted tin walls and ceiling, wood tables and ladderback chairs, and an ornate bar that was originally used in the movie *Miller's Crossing* (which was filmed here), it looks as if it's been around forever. To offset the dim lighting, there are desk lamps on all the tables for patrons who come to read, study or play games (Scrabble, chess, checkers, backgammon, and cards are available).

COFFEE: A small local roaster roasts the beans for this shop twice a week. You'll find the house blend, a basic Colombian supremo, every day, as well as a medium and dark roast, a flavored blend, and a decaf that change daily. Rue de la Course makes a great cafe mocha (and an iced version, too), and the beautiful layered latte is served in a pilsner glass. The house specialty is the Latte Delight, a latte made with the customer's choice of 23 flavorings.

FOOD: Rue de la Course claims to have the largest coffeehouse pastry selection in town, including wonderful New York-style cheesecake, huge muffins, and pecan and cinnamon rolls. They don't serve any other food.

CLIENTELE: The crowd ranges from Fortune 500 types and women in fur dropped off by their chauffeurs to grungy college students.

AZTEC STREET CAFE

317 Aztec Street
Santa Fe, New Mexico 87501 • (505) 983-9464
OPEN 7:30 A.M. TO 9 P.M. MONDAY TO THURSDAY;
7:30 A.M. TO 11 P.M. FRIDAY; 8 A.M. TO 11 P.M. SATURDAY;
8 A.M. TO 9 P.M. SUNDAY.

This unpretentious coffeehouse isn't on the radar screen for the tourists who have taken over Santa Fe, which suits the locals who hang here just fine. Located in the Guadalupe district just a few blocks from Downtown Plaza, Aztec is housed in a century-old brown adobe building that once was a residence for railroad workers. Inside there are four rough-hewn rooms (two smoking, two non-smoking), each with white adobe walls, old wood plank floors and casual seating. There's interesting artwork on the walls and a non-working but lovely fireplace in the largest room. Aztec's appeal lies in its friendly, down-home atmosphere: people look up from their newspapers and actually talk to each other.

COFFEE: Well-trained baristas serve up house coffee and espresso from Mr. Espresso, an Oakland, California, roaster. If you wish, you can also order brewed coffee from Peet's, a Berkeley, California, concern.

FOOD: Aztec serves Danish, bagels, croissants, scones, and tarts and cakes supplied by outside bakers. The menu is basic and simple: open-face egg salad sandwich, focaccia, and bruscetta.

CLIENTELE: The crowd is a mixed bag of local characters, professionals and young people.

Ah! How sweet coffee tastes! Lovelier than a thousand kisses, sweeter far than muscatel wine! I must have my coffee....

—from Johann Sebastian Bach's *Kaffee Kantate* (coffee cantata)

DOWNTOWN SUBSCRIPTION

376 Garcia Street
Santa Fe, New Mexico 87501 • (505) 983-3085
OPEN 7:30 A.M. TO 7 P.M. SUNDAY TO THURSDAY;
7:30 A.M. TO 10 P.M. FRIDAY AND SATURDAY.

From the outside, this popular hangout looks like any other Santa Fe adobe building. But inside it's a magazine lover's dream, its walls lined with newsracks carrying an outrageous selection of newspapers and "zines" for sale. Grab some reading matter and park yourself on a straight-back wooden chair; the warm, woodsy ambience won't distract you from the task at hand. But if it's a nice day, you might want to join the throngs outside on the walled-in patio, where flowering trees and bushes provide an aromatic backdrop. Located just 10 minutes from downtown in a quiet residential neighborhood, Downtown Subscription is known for its friendly staff and lack of attitude.

COFFEE: Allegro provides the house coffee, a blend of Guatemalan, Costa Rican, Mocha Java and Sumatran beans, and local roaster Ohoris supplies the espresso beans. Downtown Subscription uses Ibarra chocolate for its mochas, and double lattes and mochas are served in white ceramic bowls.

FOOD: Everything is made off the premises. The baked goods include banana bread, pumpkin-apricot bread, croissants, cinnamon rolls, muffins, biscotti, bagels, fudge espresso brownies, and cakes. For a noontime nibble, there are egg rolls, quiche, and green chili and cheese piroshki.

CLIENTELE: Tourists haven't yet discovered this coffeehouse because of its residential location. But the locals—a melange of professionals, blue collar folk and families—certainly have.

Americans drink an average of 1.8 cups of coffee a day.

BENTLEY'S HOUSE OF COFFEE AND TEA

1730 East Speedway Boulevard
Tucson, Arizona 85719 • (520) 795-0338
OPEN 7 A.M. TO MIDNIGHT MONDAY TO THURSDAY;
7 A.M. TO 1 A.M. FRIDAY AND SATURDAY;
8 A.M. TO MIDNIGHT SUNDAY.

Bentley's has been around since 1984, making it one of the old timers in Tucson's coffeehouse scene. It started out as simply an espresso bar, but over the years it has evolved into a casual restaurant serving largely vegetarian fare. Located behind the University of Arizona campus in a strip mall, it has blue and white checkered awnings and lots of windows that provide plenty of natural light. Outside, there are plastic chairs and wood tables facing the parking lot. The interior is simple and designed to appeal to students, with a large counter adorned with a colorful mural painted by employees and wood tables and old ice cream parlor chairs. There's a play area with toys for children.

COFFEE: Local roaster Tostino's supplies the coffee: a house blend, decaf, and house flavored blend, served up in heavy-duty mugs. Bentley's also makes a mean iced mocha.

FOOD: The menu leans towards vegetarian dishes, and even includes a few items for vegans. In the morning there's pecan rolls, sticky buns, scones, Danish and bagels, all supplied by outside bakers. For lunch, there's homemade soup (Mexican lime and avocado is popular) and sandwiches (try the pesto-provolone). Desserts include carrot cake and a killer chocolate decadence.

CLIENTELE: Due to its location, this is a University of Arizona hangout, but you'll also find a hefty sprinkling of townies.

CUPPUCCINOS COFFEE HOUSE

3400 East Speedway Boulevard
Tucson, Arizona 85716 • (602) 323-7205
OPEN 7 A.M. TO 11 P.M. MONDAY TO WEDNESDAY;
7 A.M. TO MIDNIGHT THURSDAY TO SATURDAY;
7 A.M. TO 10 P.M. SUNDAY.

This handsome coffeehouse, all windows and vaulted ceiling, is a perfect place to enjoy the view of the Catalina Mountains in the distance while sipping the house specialty, a double espresso with steamed milk known as the Cuppuccino. Located in central Tucson, about five miles from downtown, Cuppuccinos is a sprightly, Seattle-style cafe with concrete floors, wood tables and chairs, a retail area for coffee and tea accessories, and a counter display of green and roasted coffee beans. There's a menu board behind the counter, but the eager-to-please staff will make anything you request. Outside, there's a covered patio with wrought iron tables and plastic chairs.

COFFEE: Cuppuccinos gets its coffee from several sources, including Seattle's Torrefazione Italia for espresso and local companies Arbuckle Coffee and Wilde Rose Coffee Company. The house blend, decaf, flavor of the day and varietal of the day are served in black coffee cups; you can also order coffee made and served in a French press. Cuppuccinos has a fine selection of teas, including whole-leaf Republic of Tea.

FOOD: There's a wide selection of pastries and cookies to choose from: croissants, muffins, scones served with lemon curd, sticky buns, chocolate-dipped Florentines, and googoo bars (a chocolate chip and coconut concoction). Desserts include eclairs, brownies, creme brulee, white chocolate hazelnut cake, and chocolate cashew hazelnut torte. There's also a limited soup and sandwich menu. Saturday and Sunday mornings the chef makes omelettes at an omelette bar.

CLIENTELE: University of Arizona students eat, study and socialize here. On weekends the place fills up after the symphony, opera and local movie theaters empty out.

CHUCK SEIFERT, 59, sporting goods store owner, Tucson, Arizona:

Seifert, whose voice sounds like coffee grounds, has no sense that his new twice-daily habit of cafe sitting and coffee sipping makes him part of a nationwide trend. "Oh no, I'm just a local guy," he says. In fact, he calls his chosen cafe, Cuppuccinos Coffee House, a "joint," albeit a "classy joint. Clean, you know, modern." Before it opened across the street from his sporting goods store, he and his wife had never hung out at cafes. "We'd just go somewhere, get our coffee and get the hell out."

FAVORITE DRINK: House blend.

PER DIEM: Three. A couple in the morning, and another in the afternoon with something sweet.

WHY HE LIKES THE CAFE: "Coffee's good. I sit in the sun, get away from work, chew the fat. It's a good place to meet the manufacturers' reps. You know, private and enjoyable."

One coffee tree yields slightly less than one pound of roasted coffee a year.

APPENDIX

THE LOWDOWN ON COFFEE

For many of us, there is nothing in this world as satisfying as a cup of coffee. Its rich aroma and taste make coffee a uniquely sensual treat.

Humans have craved coffee for centuries. Originating in the African tropics, it may have been cultivated as early as 575 A.D. The original coffee drinkers steeped the leaves of the coffee plant in hot water, much like making tea, but in the mid-15th century someone discovered that you could roast the seeds of the coffee cherry. That discovery ushered in the modern era of coffee making.

There are two major species of coffee plant cultivated today: *robusta* and *arabica*.

As its name implies, *robusta* is more robust than *arabica*. It is hardier, easier to grow, resistant to disease, and has a higher plant yield. It also produces a harsher coffee with a higher caffeine content. Robusta beans are used largely in mass-produced coffees and inexpensive blends.

The *arabica* bean is the jewel in coffee's crown. Arabica beans yield the world's finest coffees, with a finer, more delicate taste and about half the caffeine of *robusta*. The *arabica* coffee plant produces the fine specialty coffees served in cafes and coffeehouses.

The *arabica* coffee plant is cultivated in the coffee belt, a strip of about 50 tropical countries that circles the globe. There are many varieties of *arabica* coffee, called varietals, most of them labeled according to the country of origin.

Because soil, climate and cultivation methods affect the taste of coffee, each region tends to produce coffee with its own particular characteristics.

Coffees from East Africa and Arabia tend to be rich in flavor, with a lot of acidity and medium to full body.

Indonesia and the Pacific produce smooth, earthy coffees with little acidity and full body. The Americas, which include South and Central America, the Caribbean and Hawaii, grow light to medium-bodied coffees with a clean, lively taste.

Coffee cultivation is a labor-intensive process. For quality coffees, laborers must hand-pick the plants' ripe cherries. Each cherry contains two seeds or beans, which are extracted using either the wet method (the cherries are soaked with water to wash away the fruity pulp, then dried) or the dry method (in which the cherries are spread out to dry in the sun, then hulled by machine).

After processing, the green beans are ready for roasting.

Roasting is a fine art, requiring a delicate hand, split-second timing and an ability to judge when the coffee bean is at its peak of flavor.

The roaster heats the green coffee beans until the water in the beans begins to steam, making the beans swell and then audibly pop. The heat causes complex polysaccharides to break down into starches and then sugars, which caramelize. Aromatic oils within the beans boil toward the surface, giving them an oily appearance.

The expansion of oils causes a second audible "crack." Along the way, the bean darkens from its original green to a rich chestnut brown. The roaster uses his or her eyes, ears and nose to judge exactly when the beans are ready. The longer they roast, the darker they become.

Roasts are classified as light, medium, dark and darkest. Despite the current vogue for dark roasts, they are not necessarily better. Some varietals are better suited to a light or medium roast. Like a vintner, the roaster uses his or her experience and knowledge to create the best product.

The roaster may combine different varietals to create blends with a more complex flavor. The most popular blend is Mocha Java.

COFFEE EXPERTS' GUIDE TO COFFEE SOURCES & ROASTS

COFFEE SOURCES AND CHARACTERISTICS

Brazil: medium-bodied with mild acidity, sweet taste and balanced aroma.

Colombia: consistently good, with good acidity, medium body, full aroma, and a sweet taste with a hint of caramel.

Costa Rica: sweetly smooth, with excellent acidity and good body.

Cuba: flat and suited for dark roasting.

El Salvador: full bodied.

Ethiopia: acidic and thick bodied.

Guatemala: well balanced, with a mild, full-bodied flavor and a distinctive smokiness.

Hawaii: medium bodied, with a superb aroma.

Honduras: acidic but with indistinct flavor.

India: full bodied, with a complex, spicy aroma and little acidity.

Kenya: sharply acidic, with an intense flavor.

Mexico: sweet and smooth, with medium acidity.

Panama: mild-flavored and heavy-bodied with good acidity.

Those varietals listed above can be roasted in a number of ways.

ROASTS

American: a light roast with a mild, sweet flavor.

Cinnamon or Vienna: a light to medium roast.

Full City: also known as regular or breakfast roast; a medium roast.

French: a dark brown roast with rich, oily beans.

Espresso: a very dark, nearly black, oily roast.

ESPRESSO

Whole volumes have been written about espresso, that dark, creamy concoction much beloved by Italians. It is a strong, concentrated drink with a bittersweet bite.

Espresso is made by forcing hot water through coffee grinds under high pressure. This method forces the maximum flavor and body out of the coffee in the shortest amount of time.

Espresso serves as the basis for most coffeehouse drinks.

Espresso Guide

Espresso Romano: espresso served with a twist of lemon.

Doppio: a double espresso.

Espresso Americano: a single espresso diluted with hot water.

Espresso Macchiato: an espresso "stained" with a touch of steamed milk.

Caffe Latte: a single espresso and steamed milk with little or no foam, poured or layered into a tall glass.

Caffe Corretto: espresso "corrected" with a shot of brandy or liqueur.

Caffe Ristretto: a "restricted" espresso, made with less water so that it's stronger and more concentrated.

Latte Macchiato: steamed, frothed milk "stained" with a dribbling of espresso.

Cappuccino: a single espresso and an equal amount of steamed milk and foam.

Cafe Mocha: a caffe latte with the addition of dark chocolate or cocoa.

Cafe Breve: a single espresso and steamed half and half.

Latteccino: a cross between a cappuccino and a latte, made with a single espresso, two parts steamed milk and one part foam.

Espresso Con Panno: espresso topped with whipped cream.

HOW TO ORDER LIKE THEY DO IN SEATTLE: A GLOSSARY OF TERMS

While there is no such thing as a right way to order the multitude of gourmet coffee drinks, it's fun to know a little lingo. In Seattle, they make an art form of it, thanks to that city's own Starbucks Coffee Company. The Starbucks chain requires its "baristas" to take about 50 hours of classroom and on-site training in coffee preparation, including the skill of "calling drinks." Would-be baristas and their instructors sit tete-a-tete practicing their translations so that they can shout them out in coffee-speak when calling the order to the employee running the espresso machine.

Here is some of the vocabulary:

skinny: non-fat milk
no-fun: decaf
ristretto: short espresso
lungo: long espresso
double: two shots of espresso
triple: three shots of espresso
quad: four shots of espresso
dry: more foam, less milk
wet: more milk, less foam
whipless: no whipped cream
short: an 8-ounce coffee drink (usually made with a single shot of espresso)
tall: a 12-ounce coffee drink (can be made with a single or double shot, depending upon customer's preference
grande: a 16-ounce coffee drink (made with two espresso shots)

Here's how they put it all together at Starbucks:

Customer: "I'd like a large latte made with two shots of espresso. And make it with 2 percent milk, please. But I don't want any foam on top. Oh, and that's decaf espresso, not caffeinated. And I'd like to drink it here, please."

Barista: "For-here decaf extra shot grande half-skim no-foam latte."

See how easy that is?

COFFEE CALORIE COUNTER

If you are watching your weight, watch what you order at the coffee bar. Some espresso drinks are low-cal, others not so.

Black coffee	8 oz.	5 calories
Espresso	0.7 oz.	5 calories
Cappuccino	8 oz.	70 calories (whole milk)
Cafe Mocha	8 oz.	180 calories

INDEX OF COFFEEHOUSES

Other Books from Aslan Publishing

Argument With an Angel

by Jan Cooper

This touching, inspirational tale is a modern parable about the good within us all and how to manifest that good daily. It stands above others in the swelling "angelology" market because of its simple message of hope and the strength it endorses. The story focuses on the relationship between an angel sent to earth to round up people to make the world a better place and a young boy named Goldstein. The message is simple, poignant, and to the point! The growing numbers of "angel fans", new age readers, Christians of every variety, and teachers alike will reach for this book.

Lovers for Life

by Daniel Ellenberg, Ph.D., M.F.C.C., and Judith Bell, M.S., M.F.C.C.

Monogamy is, and always has been, a challenge. Though our culture values long-term intimate relationships, it has failed to provide the necessary tools for achieving such relationships. Taking the position that we are all beginners who lack the proper framework for creating a lasting, passionate, and loving union, Daniel Ellenberg and Judith Bell have created a straightforward and accessible guide to successful coupling—and jubilant eroticism.

Emissary of Light

by James F. Twyman

Miracles often occur in the most unlikely places and at unexpected times. For a year, mysterious forces worked to draw Jimmy to war-torn Bosnia and Croatia. A professional musician, he thought his mission was to bring hope through the performances of *The Peace Concert.* As his journey unfolds in this captivating, real-life spiritual adventure, another mission is revealed—one that is being orchestrated by a mystical society with ancient roots, *The Emissaries of Light.* They had chosen Jimmy to bring their secret message of peace to the world

Winds Across the Sky

by Chris Foster

Every so often a novel comes along that is simple, magical, utterly unique and compelling. *Winds Across the Sky* is that kind of rare, exceptional work. Woven around the themes of ecology, recovery, male-female relationships, and other great issues of the day, Chris Foster's lean prose and poetic style make this a book that pierces the heart of the reader. This book portrays the fundamental unity of all creation in a new way and across a broader spectrum. It portrays loving communication as it occurs easily between different species and between humans and the natural world.

Other Books from Aslan Publishing

New Woman Manager

by Sharon Willen

Think of *The New Woman Manager* as your personal mentor—by your side whenever you need help with the challenges of management in today's fast-paced, often perplexing business environment. The valuable information in this book was drawn first from the author's personal experience as a young female manager in a male-dominated industry and later from the thousands of situations she has observed and analyzed in her years as a business consultant.

If You Want To Be Rich & Happy

by Robert Kiyosaki

In powerful no-nonsense language, Kiyosaki shows the root fallacies on which everything from our grading systems to our school hours are based, and demonstrates that we must make simple but radical changes in our approach if we are ever to prepare our children for the gifts of financial security and balanced, happy lives.

Intuition Workout

by Nancy Rosanoff

This is a new and revised edition of the classic text on intuition. Lively and extremely practical, it is a training manual for developing your intuition into a reliable tool that can be called upon at any time—in crisis situations, for everyday problems, and in tricky business, financial, and romantic situations. Nancy Rosanoff believes that intuition is like a muscle, it needs regular exercise to be effective. Based on her more than ten years of work with ad agency executives, corporate leaders, and

The Motion Picture Prescription

by Gary Solomon

The Movie Doctor™ Gary Solomon has loved movies his whole life. He began using movies to help his clients break through their denial and heal from their individual problems. Amazed at how successful movie therapy was, he set out to research the concept and created a comprehensive data base of movies and all their healing issues. *The Motion Picture Prescription* is a helping guide to 200 movies—each one reviewed on its own page with a cast list, a synopsis, a commentary to know what to watch for, and several healing themes for personal growth.

Other Books from Aslan Publishing

The Joyful Child

by Peggy Joy Jenkins

This book is not just for the children in your life. It is also for you. As you learn to guide your children's discovery of joy, your awareness will expand and you will grow more in touch with your own inner joy. *The Joyful Child* is both a source and a resource book. Between its covers is a wealth of ideas and activities. In addition, it is liberally sprinkled with quotations and references to lead you to a wide variety of excellent resources.

Mind, Music and Imagery

by Stephanie Merritt

Music affects our physical wellbeing, even alters our behavior, often without our being aware of it. This book illustrates the ability of music to transform our lives through simple, step-by-step exercises. The author chooses five popular works of classical music as a starting point to harness the power of music and enhance our lives. This book does more than suggest that music can be focused for our personal growth; it opens doorways to promote healing, reduce stress, inspire creativity, and enhance relationships.

More Than Just Sex

by Daniel Beaver

Author and sex therapist Daniel Beaver is on a mission to help couples keep their committed long-term relationships alive and vital. *More Than Just Sex* discusses in-depth and in a lucid and candid manner common sexual difficulties that couples experience. It explores key psychological concepts and attitudes that enhance the level of sexual pleasure and intimate involvement. By giving entrance into this intimate world, secrets are revealed to allow couples to use these concepts to create exciting and fulfilling relationships. Daniel Beaver brings together a depth and breadth of authoritative information not previously available to the general public in a single source.

Your Body Believes Every Word You Say

by Barbara Hoberman Levine

This bestselling title describes the link between language and disease. Levine's fifteen-year battle with a huge brain tumor led her to trace common words and phrases like "that breaks my heart" and "it's a pain in the butt" back to the underlying beliefs on which they are based and the symptoms they cause. With over 45,000 copies in print, this book is on it's way to becoming one of the classics of modern healing literature.

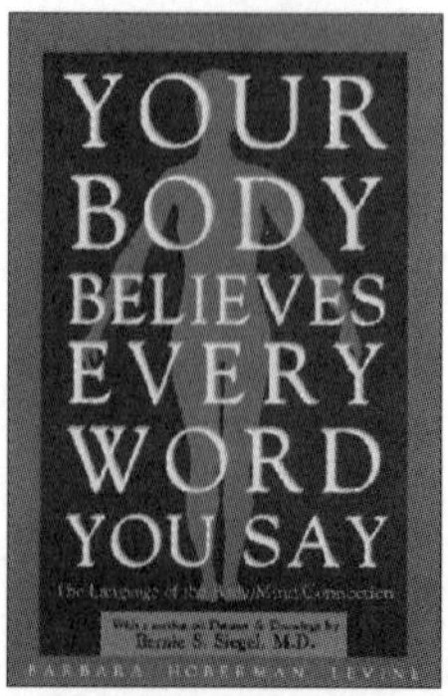

Order Form

(Please print legibly) Date ________________

Name ______________________________

Address ______________________________

City ____________________ State________ Zip ______________

Phone ______________________________

Please send a catalog to my friend:

Name ______________________________

Address ______________________________

____

Item	Qty.	Price	Amount
Argument With an Angel		$11.95	
Lovers For Life		$13.95	
Emissary of Light		$12.95	
Winds Across The Sky		$9.95	
The New Woman Manager		$14.95	
If You Want To Be Rich & Happy		$14.95	
Intuition Workout		$10.95	
Motion Picture Prescription		$12.95	
Joyful Child		$16.95	
Mind, Music and Imagery		$13.95	
More Than Just Sex		$12.95	
Your Body Believes Every Word You Say		$13.95	
		Subtotal	
		Calif. res. add 7.5% Sales Tax	
		Shipping	
		Grand Total	

Add for shipping:
Book Rate: $2.50 for first item, $1.00 for ea. add. item.
First Class/UPS: $4.00 for first item, $1.50 ea. add. item.
Canada/Mexico: One-and-a-half times shipping rates.
Overseas: Double shipping rates.

Check type of payment:

☐ Check or money order enclosed

☐ Visa ☐ MasterCard

Acct. # ______________________

Exp. Date ______________________

Signature ______________________

Send order to:
Aslan Publishing
3356 Coffey Lane
Santa Rosa, CA 95403
or call to order:
(800) 275-2606

COFCRA